DUSTERMAN

VIETNAM

Story Of

THE LAST GREAT GUNFIGHTERS
Transcripts from My Vietnam Diary and Memoirs

Written By

Joseph M. Belardo, Sr.

<u>Military Assignment:</u>
U.S. Army - 1st Field Force
Charlie Battery
1st Battalion - 44th Artillery
Automatic Weapons - Self Propelled
Twin 40mm - Dusters

Mobile Combat Team & Body Recovery
Combat Attachment to:
III Marine Amphibious Force
3rd Marine Division

Vietnam Tour of Duty
August 1967 to August 1968

DUSTERMAN

VIETNAM

Story Of

THE LAST GREAT GUNFIGHTERS

Copyright 2010 by Joseph M. Belardo, Sr.

ISBN 978-0-98022-474-0
Library of Congress 2010938264

First Edition, 2010

Edited by Samuel W. Hopkins. Jr.
Design and layout by Christine D. Kjosa

Published by the SamPat Press
Printed in the United States of America
by Lightning Source, Inc.

Correspondence and publication requests contact:

SamPat Press
1027 Timothy
Jacksonville, TX 75766
(903) 586-4488
sampatpress.com

Dedicated to the men of Charlie Battery 1st Battalion,
Automatic Weapons – Self-Propelled – 44th Artillery,
Dusters, Quad-50's, and Searchlights,
and all the Heroes who served in Vietnam.

A special recognition to my first Hero "My Father"

In Loving Memory
of
My Nephew
Scott Thomas Ribar

TABLE OF CONTENTS

PREFACE
By Chaplain Sam Hopkins

Get ready for an action packed, combat adventure story about a patriotic young man from the loving Belardo family of an Italian neighborhood in New Jersey. This G.I. named Joe served his country with honor and distinction in the most heavily decorated artillery unit in the history of the United States Army. Joe and his buddies didn't plan on being heroes; the fighting was thrust upon them by a savage enemy intent on over running their positions at any cost. If you ask these men about the frequent, memorable battles they fought in Vietnam, they will sincerely and reverently say they were just doing their job and only trying to stay alive. Despite their many decorations for bravery and valor, these mighty veterans maintain that the only heroes they know have their names on The Wall in Washington, D.C. So true, so true.

Joe is profusely modest about his tour of duty. However, the well-known Lieutenant Colonel Ollie North has nationally publicized Joe and his unit's outstanding service record on the Fox TV program Men At War. ABC television has broadcast his combat story too. Those programs were based on this publication's detailed, day-by-day, frontline battle narratives extracted from Joe's combat diary. His fascinating, introspective memoir reveals a sensitive soul's struggle to be physically and mentally strong amidst unimaginably horrible suffering and dying. He always praises the many service personnel who stood fast in the line of duty, and remains mindful of the countless sacrifices they made for God and country. As Joe has often said, "ALL GAVE SOME, AND SOME GAVE ALL." He respectfully disguises or keeps anonymous the names of people who miserably let their buddies down, or whose flawed character crumbled in the crucible of wartime's dramatic life or death struggles. Some servicemen deserve to have medals hung around their necks, and others simply deserve to be hung by the neck. Joe describes in sharp, vivid terms his experiences with the good (family, service buddies and friends), the bad (the vicious enemy constantly surrounding him), and the beautiful (the lush, green paradise known as Vietnam).

America is lucky to have men like Joe Belardo faithfully serve their country in time of war. America has been doubly blessed by his peacetime service to others too. Since his return to civilian life, Joe has unselfishly given time and tangible aid to schools, civic groups, hospitals and homes. Most of all, he helps fellow veterans in need of comfort and emotional healing. In recognition of these many good deeds, the Vietnam Veterans Association, at a national ceremony in Cape May, New Jersey, deservedly gave the prestigious "Four Chaplains" award to my dear friend and brother-in-arms, Joseph.

I should like to add a fifth chaplain's tribute to Joe's work and war record. From the perspective of a fellow combat veteran who served in a Duster unit like Joe's during the same period of time of the Vietnam War, I acknowledge with high admiration that he and his unit saw far more action than most of us. More importantly, Joe and his unit set an inspiring example of devotion to duty for all time. This old soldier salutes you, sir. As an ordained (and now retired) clergyman who has served among men and women in uniform, I am confident that Joe and his kind shall someday enter the kingdom of heaven because they have already served their time in hell. In the mean time, I pray that he and all his buddies will add many more fabulous chapters of living to their exciting chronicles begun some forty-odd years ago. Finally, as a fellow American, I offer these heartfelt sentiments to Joe and all Vietnam veterans: although you didn't hear these precious, long overdue words when you returned to the world, our nation owes you the following tribute

- Welcome Home, G.I. Thanks for a job well done.

Samuel W. Hopkins, Jr.
Chaplain (Colonel), U. S. Army, retired
Vietnam Veteran 1967-68
4th Battalion 60th Artillery, Dusters

ACKNOWLEDGEMENTS

A Simple Thank You

Over the years, I have made many relationships. I thought it was about time that I let the world know about a certain few.

To my wife, Nancy, thank you for being by my side all these years. You have worked hard to make my life simple and beautiful and full of love. We have known each other since we were fifteen. It has been a wonderful life together. I will love you forever.

To my children, Mary, Joseph and Patrick: God could not have given me better children. Thank you for always helping. You have made me the proudest dad in the world. I love you for who you are and the great adults you have become.

To my mother and father: Thank you for teaching me the values of family and friends. Thank you for your patience and love.

To my sister, Brenda, and my brother-in-law, Ken: There is nothing in my heart that can express my appreciation for the love and understanding you both have given me all my life. I will always be there for you, as you have been for me. Ken, thanks for the diary. Without it, this book could not have happened.

To Paul Fusco, my "brother": Since childhood, you have been by my side through all phases of my of life and are part of my family.

To my veteran friends: Chaplain Sam Hopkins, thank you for giving me the courage to finish this story. You are a true friend and gentleman. The world is fortunate to have a person like you. God bless you.

Lieutenant L. Steve Moore, Lieutenant Bruce Geiger, and Captain Vincent Tedesco, your leadership and concern for your men were superior to all other officers and you gave us courage. To this day you exemplify that spirit and friendship.

Sergeant Chester Sines, thank you for teaching me everything about a Duster and how to stay alive.

John "Tank" Huelsenbeck, Donald Wolfe, Earl Holt, Wally Owens, Roger Blentlinger, Norman Oss, Cleve Lanier and James "Doc" Butler, thank you for your undying friendship, weekly telephone calls, and e-mails. Most of all, thank you for risking your lives for mine.

To my other Duster, Quad-50 and Marine friends, thank you for sharing all you photographs with me. Most of all, thank you for getting me home. We are all true blood brothers.

To the rest of my family and friends, especially my cousin Michael Dellipoali: Thank you for listening to me all these years about Vietnam. Someday, when we all go and meet our "Maker", we will see each other again in heaven. Someone once told me that in the Bible there is a passage that says, "When we go to heaven, we sit at the right hand of the Father". Remember, if you want to find me, look to the left, and I'll tell you another story.

FOREWORD

While I was in the military, I was encouraged by my father and mother to keep a daily journal of my military experience. In each letter home, I included a short story of my daily experience. When I went overseas, a relative sent me a small pocket diary which encouraged me even more to keep writing.

A month after I returned home, I sat with my Father and transcribed all my paper notes and diary into one memoir. As I wrote, I shared my story with my Father. We compared my war experience with his WWII experience. My Dad had been a Sergeant in the Army and had served as General Patton's Forward Infantry Platoon and had experienced a lot of combat. It was the first time in our lives that we shared a common bond-- "WAR". Our talks also allowed both of us to unload a lot of war baggage that only fellow warriors would understand.

Finally, with the invention of the modern day computer, I copied everything that I had written on paper into my Dell. It still took years for me to have the courage to let another read my memoir. I was worried about how or what they would think of me after reading my story. I did not want to re-experience the public stoning that often befalls a Vietnam Veteran. That was another time, another place, and another Joe Belardo. A few years ago, I cut and pasted a few pages and let several of my friends and family read what I considered were my most treasured and secret thoughts. To my surprise, I was not stoned.

This is my memoir and how I saw and felt about my military experience. If you asked another with whom I served, they would either tell the same story or have their own version. It is all in retrospect and what I call "A View From the Turret."
I can only hope and pray that my memoir does these great and valiant men justice. I am proud to call them my friends and brothers. Allow me to introduce you to a group of men who represent the most courageous, brave, and heroic veterans of the Vietnam War.
They were known as Dustermen. Not only did they endure the normal

hardships of war but, during combat, were required to man their weapon in the standing or upright seated position, exposing either their entire body or upper torso. There was no room to duck, lie down, crawl, run, or hide. Dustermen were fighting the enemy eye-to-eye, face-to-face; watching every round hit its mark and seeing the enemy shooting back. The troops called it "Dueling with the Dragon". It was more like an old Wild West gunfight. These American servicemen were awarded more than 450 Medals for Valor and earned more than 1,000 Purple Hearts. I am not exaggerating when I say that they earned:

      10 - Army Presidential Unit Citations
       3 - Marine Presidential Unit Citations
      15 - Valorous Unit Awards
      11 - Meritorious Unit Commendations
       2 - Navy Meritorious Unit Commendations
      31 - Vietnam Cross of Gallantry Citations with Palm
       9 - Vietnam Civil Action Honor Medals First Class with Palm

I want you to remember where they came from, who they are, and to understand the brotherhood that bonds them.

I want you to picture the DMZ with its high mountains and lush green jungle.

I want you to envision the scream of **"INCOMING!"**, the crack of a rifle, the bang of an RPG, and the sounds and smells of war.

I want you to see the brightness of the Searchlights, the burst of the Quad-50 machine guns, and the rhythm of the Dusters' Twin 40s rapid fire.

I want you to know they were part of the ultimate ground-war fighting machine.
I want you to know that, man for man, they took more ground than they gave and earned the greatest respect of every unit to which they were

attached, as well as the grudging respect of the VC and NVA who came in front of them.

The Searchlight crews perched on the perimeter of some nameless camp, exposing themselves to mortars, rockets and sniper attacks.

The Quad-50 and Duster drivers drove down that "Road to Hell", leaving the sanctuary of their Driver's compartment to hand out ammo and retrieve the wounded and the dead, dancing between the AK-47s and hoping not to be kissed by an RPG.

The Cannoneers stood to load their guns, defying the enemy sharpshooters to hit their mark.

The Gunners and Squad Leaders picked targets and gave orders, hoping that their choice was right and would bring their crews safely back to camp.

Returning to camp only meant guard duty, mine sweeps, H&I's (Harassment and Interdictions), search and destroys, sapper attacks, more **"INCOMING!"**, and another convoy in the morning.

I want you to appreciate the support teams: cooks who fed them the best they could with the little they had; mechanics who came out in the field and kept them running at all costs; medics who would give their lives to save a friend; clerks; radio operators; ammo teams; combat chaplains who gave faith, hope and giant shoulders to lean on; and hundreds of others who were all part of the best fighting group in Vietnam. I can't say enough about the NCOs (Non-Commissioned Officers) and the officers who lived and fought beside them. They directed them with concern, understanding and military professionalism, as proven by the amount of unit citations and minimal number of casualties versus the number of battles fought.

No matter how history was written or what the journalists said, when these men left Vietnam they knew they had militarily won the war. They won all the battles. Then, someone forfeited their war.

We Dustermen have a simple saying…

"Always Remember – We Are Somebody".

A SPECIAL THANK YOU
TO SAM, CHRISTINE,
LISA, MIKE,
& NANCY

THIS BOOK WOULD
HAVE NEVER HAPPENED
WITHOUT ALL YOUR
HARD WORK, DEDICATION,
AND LOVE.

THANK YOU!
JOE

Joe Belardo Vietnam 1967 age 20

Chapter 1: UNCLE SAM WANTS YOU

On October 24, 1966, I was drafted into the United States Army. Because I was from New Jersey, I was sent to Fort Dix. Like all new GIs (Government Issues), I got the standard issue haircut, boots and uniform. To my surprise, we were loaded on an airplane and shipped out to Fort Hood, Texas for Basic Training in Battery C, 1st Battalion, 78th Artillery. After landing, we were then loaded on buses and transported to Fort Hood. As the bus drove through the main gate at Fort Hood, we saw a life-sized statue of Elvis Presley. The bus driver told us that Fort Hood was considered the home of Elvis Presley and that Elvis had donated a lot of recreation and restaurant places for soldiers to enjoy.

When the bus finally came to a halt, we were introduced to the traditional "Welcome to the Military". It was like the bus had been struck by lightning. Drill Instructors jumped into our bus, yelling and screaming for us "termites" to get off their buses. Their language was an assembly of operatic curse words, transformed into a dialogue of songs that only a Drill Instructor after many years of training troops could sing. It was beyond anything any of us had ever heard or experienced. Yet, we all knew exactly what they wanted us to do. As instructed, we emptied the bus in seconds and formed three equal rows of fifteen, twenty feet from the bus. One of the soldiers took out a tape measure and measured the distance from the bus to our first row of men. Holding the tape high in the air, he screamed that we were a bunch of "blind asshole dickheads" and could not measure dog shit. We all laughed and that made him go wild. At the top of his lungs with his eyes bulging out of his head, screaming a slur of profanities, he ordered us to "hit it" and give him "twenty". Only those who had played sports knew that he wanted us to do pushups. I nudged the guy next to me to follow my lead and hit the ground. We gave him his twenty and jumped back up. Those who did not follow his instructions were ordered to run in circles, screaming that they were "assholes" and "pussies", and wanted to live on a diet of shit and used condoms. Finally, after all the yelling and screaming, we were introduced to our personal Drill Instructor or "DI", a soldier named Sergeant Dillard.

Compared to a lot of the other guys, I was in good physical shape. I had played sports in high school and boxed on the P.A.L. boxing team, so I was better prepared for the rigors of boot camp. I thought that boot camp, with all its running, calisthenics, marching, shooting, teamwork and military protocol, was a fantastic experience. We were now soldiers and being retrained to the military way of life, which also included cleaning the bathrooms or as they called them, "latrines". All of us took turns at this job, which included using a combination of mops, brushes, sponges and toothbrushes, making our latrine shine until our DI could see his reflection and be proud of what he called his "girls".

After our graduation from Boot Camp, we were given a two week leave. I flew home and surprised my parents, family and friends for Christmas. While on leave I asked my high school sweetheart, Nancy, to marry me. We agreed that we would get her an engagement ring and make wedding plans on my next leave. Christmas break was great, seeing all my friends and relatives, and especially the Christmas Italian feast. I returned to Fort Hood and was assigned to 1st. Battalion, 16th Artillery for my AIT (Advanced Individual Training). In AIT, I was trained as a rocket assembler for an old surface-to-ground, high-explosive or small nuclear warhead rocket called "Honest John". Our First Sergeant was named Johnson. Sgt. Johnson was quite a character. In our first formation as new AIT trainees, the good old Sergeant did an alphabetical roll-call of names. We were instructed to take one step forward as our names were read. Loud and clear he called: Allen, Allsworth, Bailey, Bardone, Bellarah, Block, Ellis, Grinner, Gunesch, Harris, Raymond, Roundtree, Smith, Truman, Upchurch, Waite and Woods. As he called out each name, he quickly stepped in front of the person, giving each one of us the once over. At the end of roll call, I and two others did not have their names called. What happened next was something totally unexpected. One at a time, the Sergeant went up to us, just pointed at us, and made the following loud announcement, "As long as you are in my Battery, Treemont will be called Truman because he looks like good old President Truman, Shapiro will be called Smith because he looks like Buffalo Bob Smith from Howdy Dowdy, and this

Belardo guy will be called Bellarah because I don't like names ending in "O". Do you understand me, ladies?! Do you get my message?!" To which we responded, "Yes, First Sergeant!" "By the way, Bellarah, you are I-talian?" "Yes, Sergeant!" as I snapped to attention. "I-talians do know how to plant a garden?" "Yes, Sergeant!" "Starting tomorrow, on the left side of my building, you will make me a garden. I want my garden to be fifty feet wide by fifty feet long. I want two rows each of tomatoes, peppers, eggplants, lettuce and string beans. I'll get together with you next week and give you the rest of my list. It's January, so you can work two hours a day getting it ready for spring planting." I just stood there in disbelief. With that he walked to the front of the formation, slowly turned, and in his booming voice said "If I catch any of you Mother Fuckers fuckin' with my garden or giving Bellarah any shit, I'll shoot you myself! Do you fagots understand me?!" "Yes, First Sergeant!" "Formation dismissed."

Army life was easy and my only concern was keeping the Sarge happy with his new garden, as it gave me a few extra privileges. The First Sarge got me my own ¾ ton truck so I could run all his errands. My friends were jealous. Besides my daily chores for the Sarge, I was being trained as an Honest John Rocket assembler. The highlight of our assembling was placing the rocket on a launching rail truck and doing firepower shows for high-ranking officers and state dignitaries at the end of each month. The Honest John launching was the grand finale. Shot without warhead at some unseen target thirty-five miles away, it was so fast that a standard instamatic camera could not catch it in flight. You would hear the launcher yelling the countdown: 10, 9, 8, 7, 6, 5, 4, 3, 2, 1, FIRE! There were a few popping sounds, a flash, then a giant flame out the rear of the rocket that burned all the paint off the launching truck. In a blink the rocket was gone, leaving behind a cloud of dust and a loud explosion as it broke the sound barrier, making everyone jump and scream. It was fantastic!

I liked military life and thought strongly about making it a career. At first I thought of going to OCS (Officers Candidate School). All of the officers graduating from OCS went straight to Vietnam and that immediately changed my mind about pursuing that path. My goal was to get a college education from Uncle Sam and then, if I had to go overseas, it might not have to be to Vietnam. Through the encouragement of two cousins who were career military, or what they called "Lifers", I then applied for a military appointment to West Point through the Fort Hood Base Commander. After a series of tests, I was put on a waiting list for prep school in Maryland and, if I did well, I'd go on to West Point. Since I was not going to advance with the other soldiers on Honest Johns, I remained a Private E-2, the lowest of military personnel.

Without the advancement of rank, I got all the menial tasks. Weekly, I would have KP (Kitchen Police). KP meant working in the barrack's kitchen and dining area known as the "Mess Hall". I would learn to clean off plates, wash dishes, peel potatoes by the thousands, wash floors, clean stoves and ovens, load milk into the milk machines, clean out garbage cans, and the nasty job of cleaning out the giant grease traps.

Another one of my weekly jobs was GD (Guard Duty). GD was an all night task that rotated on and off every two hours. Most of the time, we guarded military equipment and buildings. Prior to GD, the duty officer of the night held what they called "Guard Mount". The officer inspected your clothes, your rifle for cleanliness, and asked a series of questions. If you passed inspection and answered the questions correctly, the officer named you "Colonel's Orderly." As Colonel's Orderly, you got two days off with no duty. I learned that none of the guys liked KP or guard duty, especially on Fridays or weekends, so we would swap days. Our Duty Sergeant did not mind as long as he had enough soldiers for each duty detail. Each night I studied military handbooks and learned the answers to all the duty officer's questions, hoping to be named Colonel's Orderly. I now had my week planned: Fridays KP, Friday night GD, answer all the officer's questions, and have the weekend off. It was a great plan that would give me the weekends off so I could fish the Texas lakes for bass.

Once a week I demonstrated shooting techniques for the new guys taking basic training. I had to show them the various shooting positions: standing, kneeling, sitting-cross legged like an Indian, and the prone position. I then took a shot or two at targets set at various distances, so they knew where to shoot. Twice a month I would demonstrate the shooting of a .45 pistol for the officers in training. In July 1967, I was issued orders to go to Vietnam. I thought they had made a mistake because I was still on the waiting list for prep school. Plus, I only had the rank of E-2 and you had to be an E-3 (PFC/Private First Class) to go to Vietnam. The First Sergeant told me that my dreams of going to West Point would have to wait and he instantly made me a PFC. Uncle Sam needed me in Vietnam. He thanked me for the great I-talian garden and wished me well. Smiling, as we shook hands, I palmed his desk memento and placed it in my pocket. It was a small cannon shell casing with our unit crest 1st/16th on one side. My friend, Doug Stamp, took over as gardener. He wasn't even I-talian.

I had come from a long line of veterans and quickly realized the idea of fighting communism and oppression was something that seemed natural. Freedom was the right I was born to defend. I would go to Vietnam and serve my country proudly. As I left Fort Hood, I could hear the new GIs going through boot camp, singing and marching in cadence to "Kill a Commie for Mommy".

The Army gave me a thirty-six day leave. I never told my parents I was coming home or even going to Vietnam. I arrived at Newark Airport about 9:00 p.m. and began hitchhiking to Plainfield. I lived in South Plainfield, the next town over, and knew that, if I got to Plainfield, a friend or cousin hanging out at the local diner would take me home. I was picked up by a kind stranger who told me he could not drop me off where I wanted because he had heard on the radio that Plainfield was in the throes of a race riot. Instead, he dropped me off about a half-mile from the diner. The side streets were barricaded and, as I casually walked down the main street in the center of town, I could hear gun shots in the distance. As the song said, "The Times They Are A-Changin'."

Leave was great. I got engaged to my Nancy. My friends and family gave me non-stop parties. Inside, I've always felt guilty about how, without warning, without softening the news, I went home and told my parents, sister, girlfriend and relatives that I was going off to war. They were shocked and cried a lot. I pinned a poster of Allen Ginsburg on my parents' living room wall. Ginsberg was dressed as Uncle Sam with his index finger pointing at you, with a caption that read "Uncle Sam Wants You". I told my family "We'll take that down when I come home." On my last day, we all sat in the airport together. We are a close family, giving hugs, kisses, and the reassurance that all would be fine and I'd be home before we knew it. It's only one year. I did not realize how difficult it was to say goodbye and maybe what could be our final farewells. Taking turns, I hugged my mother, father, my sister Brenda and brother-in-law Ken. I saved Nancy for last and gave her a big hug and kiss. I held her face for a brief moment, looked into her eyes, kissed her forehead and told her I loved her. Holding back a few goodbye tears, I slowly turned and walked away. I was really going to miss her. My original intent was to marry her, but I knew better. I did not want her to be a young widow.

As I walked to the plane, my father yelled my name and came running to me. My father, a strong-spirited, hard Italian man, was calling after me, "I have something for you!" I stood there bewildered, not knowing what he was talking about or going to do. He slowly took out his wallet and removed a small square of red cloth and held it firmly in his hard, callused, steelworker's hand. He said, "You can borrow this for one year. My mother gave me this when I went off to war with Patton. I carried it across Europe and it brought me home. Your grandmother gave it back to me when she was dying. When you come home, I'll be the first to meet you and it will be the first thing you give me." He pressed the little red square into my hand and muttered, "Now get out of here." To my surprise, the little red square was an old religious scapular. I placed it in my wallet and held back my tears. At the same time, Louis Block, another local boy and good friend, was saying his goodbyes to his family. We had gone through boot camp together and advanced training, and were now boarding the plane together for Oakland, California and then Vietnam. Lou and I caught up in our own emotions about leaving our family, said nothing to each other for the first hour of the plane ride. Together in California, we spent our last night of freedom hanging out with the Hippies at the infamous corner of Haight and Ashbury in San Francisco, before reporting to Oakland's debarkation center for Vietnam.

On August 21, 1967, I arrived in Bien Hoa, Vietnam for assignment to an artillery unit in Saigon. The twenty-seven hour flight from California to Vietnam was long and tiring. I thought it was generous that our government had chartered Braniff Airlines to bring its troops to Vietnam. It was a long flight and, after the plane touched down, we all jumped out of our seats readying ourselves to depart the plane. We did not know what to expect. Through the windows, we could only see a few buildings with soldiers and civilians milling around. As the airplane's crew opened the exit door, the noon heat of Vietnam came pouring into the plane. Instantly, the plane went from a comfortable 70 degrees to an unbearable 100 degrees of suffocating humidity. Men at the front of the line started getting lightheaded from the drastic change. Our nostrils perked open to the smells of our new home as we all gasped for air.

After arriving at the Army deportation center in Bien Hoa, we were reissued orders and sent to the seaport town of Nha Trang. A fellow soldier, Steve Harris, and I volunteered for office duty. All we did for three days was sign people in and out of this Army Transfer Center. It was a cake job. We spent the afternoons at the beach. Nha Trang was beautiful and Vietnam seemed like a tropical paradise. The Duty Sergeant told us they were looking for limo drivers for military dignitaries. We all had great hopes of becoming those limo drivers. That evening the Viet Cong hit the airport with mortars. The sound whistling over our heads brought us back to our war-torn reality. It was our first war experience and we had no idea what to do or where to go. Frightened out of our minds, we hid behind some steel storage containers. Our only defense was some giant Jim Bowie knives we had each purchased that day at the local PX (Post Exchange store). We stood there, brazen in the night, thrusting our knives into the shadows and yelling, "Commie Bastards, try and kill us! We'll kill some of you before you get all of us!" We all laughed, with fear in our voices, as we spoke of holding "the Cong" at bay.

The morning of our fourth day, the Duty Sergeant told us to "saddle up". We were being re-assigned to an Army mobile artillery unit called the 1st Battalion (Automatic Weapons) (Self-Propelled), 44th Artillery (1/44th). Our new unit was attached to the Third Marine Division stationed along the DMZ (Demilitarized Zone) in the northern most sector of "I" Corps. We were body replacements for an ambush that had taken place on August 21st. The Sergeant chuckled as he said, "Welcome to the Marines, hope you make it back." There were twenty-four of us from the Honest John Missile Training Unit to arrive in Nam. I wondered how many of us would be going home.

On the way to the 1/44th, we slept on an LZ (Landing Zone) pad in Da Nang. When we awoke, we found the local villagers had stolen my bags and the bags of two others. This was an omen of my tour to come in Vietnam. I was naive enough to have left all my orders, papers, and personnel record information in my bags. I was really mad at myself for being so stupid and trusting.

We finally boarded a C-130 cargo plane and headed to Dong Ha, the most northern airport in South Vietnam. The C-130 was packed like sardines with Marines and us few Army personnel. We sat in rows on the floor, with our backs to the front of the plane. Each row of men sat with the next man between his legs. We all held tight to nylon cargo straps secured to the floor. The rear cargo door was opening as we made our final steep decent towards the runway. The first loud explosion was heard as NVA (the enemy, North Vietnamese Army) artillery tried to blow the plane out of the sky. The plane shook violently as the NVA artillery followed it to the ground. Rays of sunlight peaked through the hundreds of holes made in the plane's skin from the exploding bombs. Men started praying, yelling, screaming, and bleeding. The plane seemed to be heading straight to the ground. I thought we were going to crash and die in a ball of fire. Another explosion was followed by another and then another. More holes in the plane, more blood, and more pieces of America's Best splattered everywhere. We were covered in smears of red and body parts I had never seen before. My friend, Louis Block, who was sitting between my legs, started screaming, "I'm hit! I'm hit!" As he turned to face me, I could see a long thin piece of shrapnel sticking out of the center of his forehead. It looked like an Indian headdress feather. Head wounds bleed profusely, so his head and face were instantly covered in blood. I started screaming with him. I yelled so loud, it made no sound. Our screams could not be heard over the loud explosions, the roar of the engines, and the crescendo of fellow soldiers and Marines scrambling and praying for their lives. Louis was lucky it had only broken the skin and not punctured his skull. He was yelling, "Take it out! Take it out!" It was terrible seeing him with that piece of shrapnel sticking out of his head, so I obliged him, pulled it out, applied pressure, and we held each other tight. Vietnam had gone from beautiful to ugly in just a few seconds.

On touchdown, the C-130 quickly slowed to a slow roll and we were ordered to jump off the moving plane through the rear cargo door. The excited flight crewman at the cargo door threatened to shoot and throw us off the plane screaming, "My plane is worth more than your sorry asses! Get the hell off my plane, before I shoot you off!" As instructed, we grabbed our bags and jumped out the back of the plane. Holding onto Louis, I made a mad dash to safety, sprinting, stumbling and crawling to a small building on the north side of the runway. For the first time we were running for our lives, frightened beyond anything we had ever experienced. The C-130 never stopped, but did a fast U-turn and hastily flew back to Da Nang, its wheels almost hitting the men it had strewn all over the runway.

"INCOMING!" A volley of enemy artillery shells started landing all around us. Crazy with a new kind of fear, we all dived into a very long trench about five feet deep by three feet wide that was filled to the top with smelly, muddy water. Only moments before, we had spoken of our bravery and how we wouldn't jump into that nasty looking ditch. As I stood chest deep in the condemned water, I could feel something wiggling under my feet. In my frantic haste to take cover, I had jumped on top of my friend, Frank Bardone. I almost drowned poor Frank. We were all so nervous and jumpy, it didn't matter. Lou pointed to some guys running along the runway and saw them disappear into some kind of underground bunker. Leaping from the muddy water, Lou and I sprinted to the bunker. Finally inside and trembling with fear, we tried to regroup. The other guys in the bunker tried to reassure us. Lou asked me for a cigarette because his got wet. I took off my helmet and reached inside for my Tareytons. My hand was shaking so much, I could not hand Louis a cigarette. They just seemed to be jumping out of the pack on their own and landing on the floor. Finally, we lit up, took a big drag and both exclaimed "Holy Shit!"

We were the new guys they called "Newbees." The experience, natural to war, was only a taste of what was to come. Being wet, hot, cold, or half-drowned would soon be the least of our problems. By the end of our first day on the famous DMZ, we would hide from the enemy artillery five more times. "Welcome to the Vietnam Conflict."

Private Joe Belardo,
Advanced Individual Training Graduate

Honest John Rocket

Nancy and I got engaged before I deployed to Vietnam.

Belardo family religious scapular that was carried by my father in WW-II and me in Vietnam.

U.S. Army "Duster" unit attached to 3rd Mar Div

It's a long way from Fort Bliss, Texas and the Oro Grande, New Mexico desert training area, but the 1st Battalion (Automatic Weapons) (Self Propelled) of the 44th Artillery Regiment made it.

The Army battalion is now settled in the Dong Ha base perimeter and adds its tremendous firepower to the 3d Marine Division. The battalion is unique in that it has the "Ocelots" of Battery G, (50 CAL MG) 65th Artillery attached as a machine-gun element.

The battalion has had a long and proud heritage of the 44th Artillery which it now carries to the DMZ. Twenty-six battle streamers and two presidential citations add body to the battalion colors; ranging from World War I through World War II campaigns and the Korean Conflict. Reactivation at Fort Bliss, Texas, in March 1966 was followed by intensive basic and advanced unit training at Oro Grande Range Camp, neighboring White Sands Missile Range, New Mexico, in preparation for deployment to the Republic of Vietnam.

The 44th brings into combat weapons that have been re-established in the Army arsenal; M42, twin 40mm gun, mounted on a light track chassis, with latest modifications, and M55, 50 Caliber (Quad 50) mount machine-gun. The M42 has been known as the "DUSTER" since its conception, and has proved the title well earned in dry weather. The M55 "Quad" type machinegun earned the title "WHISPERING DEATH" from the Chinese Communists during the Korean Conflict. Both have a tremendous firepower as a ground support weapon and still maintain the ability to fire against low level air targets in the Dong Ha base defense.

I had just arrived in Vietnam in this picture.
The next day I was put on a plane like the one in this photo
and flown to a place called Dong Ha.

DMZ
(Demilitarized Zone)

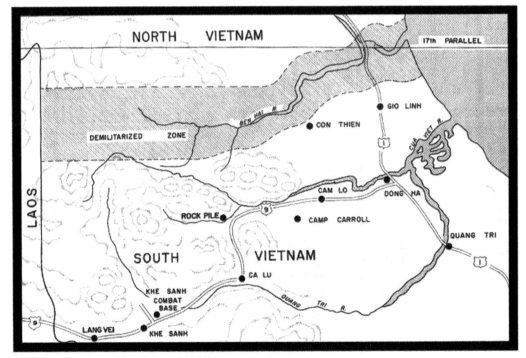

Belardo's deployment area in Vietnam

Chapter 2: THE DUSTER GUNFIGHTER

At 1st/44th Headquarters in Dong Ha, I was told not to worry because all my records would be reconstructed and placed in proper order. I was still concerned that, without my records, I really didn't exist in the military. For some stupid reason, I did not want them to lose me or misplace me.

We all thought we were going to a standard artillery unit on the DMZ to be trained how to shoot some kind of big cannon over a hill at the unseen enemy. I should have known better, since they told us the 1st/44th used some kind of self-propelled automatic-weapon and was attached to the Third Marine Division.

The officer in charge of our training explained to us that the 44th was comprised of Twin 40mm Dusters, an attachment of Quad-50 machine guns mounted on 2½ ton trucks, and Searchlights mounted on the back of jeeps, all incorporated into the Marine Corps as their mobile combat team and body recovery unit. It was our job to provide perimeter and convoy security, daily guard duty, evening firing of Harassment and Interdiction missions, search and destroy missions, body recovery, or anything else the Marines required. All of our group would be trained and shipped to different combat batteries along the DMZ. We looked at each other in wonderment and disbelief. The officer then turned us over to his Training Sergeant.

The Sergeant first introduced us to the Quad-50 machine gun. The Quad had four 50 caliber machine guns mounted on a very small motorized turret that one man, the Gunner, could sit in and shoot. The turret was then mounted on the rear deck of a 2½ ton truck. There were two Loaders and one Driver. The top deck of the truck was loaded with two layers of ammo cans. The Quad-50 shot up to 1,500 rounds per minute. We had a quick four hour lesson on the Quad, each taking a turn loading, unloading and shooting the Quad. I could not believe the firepower this weapon had when you shot all four guns at once. It was a blaze of bullets, ripping the earth to shreds, including anything in its way. We all hoped that we would be the Gunner, sitting inside the mini-turret, squeezing the triggers and blazing away at the charging enemy. At the end of the four hour training lesson, the Sergeant told us that he just wanted us to be familiar with the weapon in case we had to use them in combat and that we were being assigned to Dusters. We still had not seen a Duster and had no idea what he was talking about.

Instead of being trained on cannons that shot long range over hills at the unseen enemy, we were now introduced to a small tank-like weapon that shot directly at the enemy. This little tracked vehicle had two small cannon barrels (Twin 40s) and was called a "Duster."

After three days of training, we learned that the Duster crew was comprised of a five man fighting team: a Squad Leader, a Driver, a Gunner and two Cannoneers. The Duster had the same Twin 40mm Bofors ack-ack cannons that were mounted on Navy ships and were used to shoot down enemy airplanes. The twin machine gun cannons, with open turret, were re-mounted onto a small modified Walker Bulldog tank chassis and renamed the "Duster". The four men who sat in the small open turret were only protected by a thin ¼ inch thick armor plate that gave no adequate protection from enemy ground forces. The top edge of the turret was only twenty-four inches high and exposed the crew to enemy fire. Their head, chest and arms were totally unprotected. Upper head and chest wounds were quite common. The two Cannoneers had to stand to load the machine gun-like cannon shells into the clip-fed high-speed loaders, or shoot the M60 machine gun or their personal weapon, exposing themselves to increased danger. The Gunner sat to the left of the cannons, with head and chest exposed, and was responsible for raising and lowering the guns and shooting the auto-cannons. The Squad Leader sat to the right of the cannons, with head and chest exposed, traversing the turret left to right and giving target acquisitions.

The Driver sat below the turret and was responsible for daily track maintenance. His responsibilities also included radio communications, calling in and coordinating artillery and air strikes while under attack.

During combat, the Driver was forced to leave the confines of his compartment and distribute ammunition stored inside the track to the men in the turret. It was also the Driver's job to make sure the enemy did not get close to or breach the Duster. The Squad Leader, Gunner, and Driver wore radio-equipped plastic helmets for constant communication. The two Cannoneers wore standard-issue helmets. Because of the lack of officers, the Squad Leaders were totally in command of the Duster with the Driver being second in command. On the Duster, there was no room to hide or run. The crew had to stand and fight, brazenly defying the enemy to kill them.

The Training Sergeant barked, "This, 25 tons of steel is not a tank. It is a track vehicle, type M42A1, better known as a Duster. When some Marine General saw us shoot at Fort Bliss, he had Congress assign our sorry asses to the Marine Corps. The Dusters and Quad-50s are the meanest, toughest, mother-fuckin' killing machines in all Vietnam."

We would soon learn that the crew of a Duster seldom saw their Battery Headquarters or an officer. Because the Squad Leaders were in charge of the Dusters, our trainer called it a "Sergeant's War". We were orphaned out to Marines or other outfits scattered across the DMZ and received most of our orders via radio. Each day started an hour before sunup with a mine sweep along part of the road. Then we would return to base to take a group of Marines on a combat or body recovery mission, or a convoy to an isolated oasis called a "Combat Base".

Convoy duty was dangerous and nerve-racking. During World War II and the Korean War, U.S. convoys operated mainly behind enemy front lines with virtual impunity. Things were different in Vietnam. You never held the ground you fought. You never advanced from town to town as you defeated the enemy. There were no front lines and your permanent base camps were prime enemy artillery targets.

Ambushes were a constant threat along all supply routes. Ambushes posed a serious logistics problem since trucks provided most of the supplies for inland installations and combat bases. Normally, on convoys or search and destroy missions, the lead Duster (at or near the front) covered the left side of the road while the rear Duster covered the right side. The roads we traveled were usually in the valleys of the mountainous northern terrain where we lived, thus making us easy targets. Convoy duty was like being in a shooting gallery, except we were the targets, "the sitting ducks". Dusters, caught in an ambush, pulled off the road, traversed their guns and provided covering fire. The remainder of the convoy accelerated to escape the Kill Zone. The tactic was effective, but it meant Duster crews spent eternities in the Kill Zone. Sometimes ambushes would overwhelm even the firepower of the Dusters. When this happened, a reactionary force would hopefully roll to the rescue from one of the nearby base camps.

Duster crews from the 1st Battalion (Automatic Weapons) (Self-Propelled), 44th Artillery were stationed at Dong Ha, Gio Linh, Con Thien, Cam Lo, Camp J.J. Carroll, Khe Gio Bridge, Rockpile, Ca Lu, LZ Stud, Khe Sanh, Quang Tri and a dozen other outposts, reaching as far south as Hue. Their total effectiveness was reduced by the vast amount of territory they had to patrol.

The Duster shot two hundred-forty 40mm high explosive cannon shells per minute. It had M60 machine guns, LAW's rocket launchers, hand-grenades and the crew's personal weapons. With a top speed of about fifty miles per hour, it was the perfect mobile ground weapon. It was an awesome weapon for war, fast and accurate, with an effective firing range of three straight miles. Each cannon shell travelled at twice the speed of sound and upon impact had a one hundred foot shrapnel killing field. After three miles, if the target wasn't hit, the warhead would self-detonate into what was called "flak". The Duster was originally meant to shoot down airplanes and instead was used against enemy ground forces. Its firepower was more than two companies of infantry. When firing, it looked like the grand finale at the 4th of July fireworks, but ten times louder and a hundred times more dangerous. It was the Army's gift to the Marines, a mobile five-man combat team and body recovery unit. It meant death and destruction for the enemy and was one of America's ultimate ground weapons. Basically, it was just two big machine gun cannons mounted on a small, tracked vehicle…a human killing machine.

Dusters and Quad-50s were a lethal combination and were considered the most devastating ground weapons in Vietnam. Because of their fire power, they were hunted by every enemy sharpshooter. Destroying one of these weapons was the dream of every NVA soldier.

After three days of "OJT" (on the job training) on a weapon that none of us had ever seen or used, we were told we were ready for combat and would be assigned to our respective Combat Batteries. We were now official "Dustermen". Our small group of "Newbee0073" was taken to the Chapel for a short church service before departing headquarters and going to our new positions. On the wall of the Chapel was a plaque listing the names of those already killed or missing in action from our unit. The Chaplain slowly read their names: Wright, Ford, Croom, Fox, Teatsworth, Wilkerson, Royster, Thompson, Atkins, Henry, Evans, Lewis, Cribbs, Schneider, Pendergrass, Gerber, Valenzuela, Watson, Weigert, Baldoni……losing track of the names as he read, I prayed he would never have to read my name.

We didn't have to guess to which Battery most of us would be sent. Two of the men went to "A" (Alpha) Battery, one to "B" (Bravo) Battery and one stayed at Headquarters. The rest of us were sent to "C" (Charlie) Battery as body replacements for their August 21st battle.

A guy named John "Tank" Huelsenbeck ordered us to load onto a 2½ ton truck. As we got on the truck, he gave each of us one of the KIA (killed in action) names that were listed on the Chapel wall. He grabbed my arm and told me I was now Billy Watson and I better not let him down. I just stared at him and nodded my head in agreement. Christ, I better live up to this Billy Watson guy's reputation. Without any personal weapons or the knowledge of where we were going, we drove alone without escort down a dusty dirt road called Route 9 to a place someone called "Carroll." This we were told was "SOP" (standard operating procedure) and our initiation to the DMZ. I could not help but think that this Route 9 looked nothing like Jersey's good old Route 9. I couldn't believe how casually Tank drove down this long dusty road. The soldier who rode shotgun in the cab had handed each of us one hand grenade. He laughed as he told us that, if something happened, to pull the pin and kill ourselves, because if the NVA caught us, they would cut off our balls and stick them in our mouths…another new kind of fear.

Heading west from Dong Ha on Route 9, we passed the Vietnamese relocation settlement of Cam Lo and then slowly ascended into the area called the Dong Ha Mountain ridge line. We finally made a hard left turn and headed up another long winding dirt road to Carroll. They all must have gotten a good Christian education on that ride, as I recited out loud all the prayers I had learned as a young boy.

At Carroll we were finally issued M-16 rifles and ammunition from a guy named Mike Romanski. After inspecting my M-16, I realized that the barrel had a slight bend. I went back to the supply room and asked for an exchange. Romanski just shrugged his shoulders, smiled and said he had issued me a good rifle and, if I wanted another rifle, what did I have to trade. I had to give him a pack of cigarettes to get my choice of rifles. Tank then brought us to the Command Post Bunker where we were introduced to Captain Morgan, Lieutenant Amerman, the First Sergeant Slater, equipped with a handlebar mustache, and our Platoon Leader, Lieutenant Moore.

Captain Morgan welcomed us to Camp J.J. Carroll named after a Marine officer who gave his life defending his Marines. Carroll was centrally located along Route 9 and situated on top of a high, flat-topped mountain overlooking the DMZ and several combat bases in the area. He also told us that Carroll was known as "Artillery Hill" because of all the heavy duty, short and long range cannons located on the base. He told us that Carroll's artillery included 105, 106, 155 and 175 millimeter cannons, 8 inch cannons and an assortment of mortar platoons. Carroll's artillery could protect all bases up to thirty-four miles away. Plus, it was the home and central jumping-off point for all the Marine units in the area. He then gave us another brief description of Duster life and how we would interact with the Marines. Lt. Amerman and the First Sergeant each gave a short speech and then turned us over to our Platoon Leader Lt. Steve Moore.

Moore now separated us into our respective new MOSs (Military Occupational Specialties). He was shocked and upset that his new men had no formal stateside military training on a Duster. Four of the men were assigned to "C" Battery Headquarters, working in the motor pool or communications. The rest of us went directly onto "tracks" (Dusters). Moore asked if any of us knew how to drive a Duster. I told him I knew how to drive a bulldozer and I instantly became a Driver. I didn't mind and thought it beat being a Cannoneer. Gun Bunnies, as we called them, had to stand and load the cannons. Since the turret was high off the ground, it made them an even greater target. I didn't think being a Gun Bunny would be safe. I would soon learn that no job was safe.

As I listened to Moore give his lecture about what he expected of us and what life would be like in base camp, on the road, and in combat, I could not help but think this was going to be like the gunfight at the OK Corral and that I was going to be another Wyatt Earp. Maybe trying to get from base to base strung out across the DMZ would be more like storming Omaha Beach and Iwo Jima combined. All I knew was this "jungle dirt highway" he called Route 9 sounded real scary. He expressed, over and over, how the Duster was a crew-served weapon and that her crew had to stand to fight the enemy. "Since there is no room on a Duster to duck or hide, you will always see who is shooting at you and you will also see who you kill." At all cost we had to protect ourselves, the troops in our charge, and the Duster's virtues from all enemy intruders. He expected his men to rise to the occasion, stand tall and make Charlie Battery 1st/44th proud and nothing less. I thought it was interesting that he referred to the Duster as a woman. He ended with a prayer. Moore's speech made the Duster come alive and the war a reality.

Of all the officers I got to know, Lt. Moore would earn the most respect from his men. Moore thought like the men who rode the roads. He knew from early encounters with the NVA how to use the Duster firepower to our advantage, what to do and what not to do in a firefight. Getting in too close didn't always mean victory. It always gave me a feeling of relief when Moore was in the TC's (Track Commander's) hatch. The TC hatch was an additional individual seat to the right of the Driver. We all felt Moore was not there for the glory, like some other officers. Moore was there for his men. I would steal knowledge from this man by listening, learning and adapting. The only hard part about fighting on the road with Moore was that we were quite sure we would be the last ones back to camp after a firefight. Moore always accounted for his men and the Marines we supported. Moore never knew that returning back to camp last from a battle meant, to the men at the camp, that we had kicked some NVA butt and were one of "Moore's Road Warriors". Surviving the battles gave us courage and gave courage to the men who never rode the road. It gave us another reason to "saddle up" and escort the next convoy down the infamous Route 9.

To my surprise, I was sent immediately to the First Track Position directly in front of the Mess Hall at Camp Carroll. My new home was a "bunker", a 9 foot cube with only one door, no windows, and constructed from sandbags and old ammunition cans. This hole in the ground had only candles for light and an outside outhouse they called the "shitter." Little did I know, a bunker would be the best home I'd have over the next year. If we didn't have a bunker to live in, we slept under the stars or under the Duster.

I was introduced to my new combat team: Dieter, Lanier, Green, and Musso. Their Driver, a soldier named Louis Calya, who was going home in a few days, would be training me to be the new Driver. The men welcomed me with a traditional hot meal of C-Rations (meals in a can). Stateside, I had only eaten C-Rations once, which we cooked in the can on a tiny field stove. Cleve Lanier insisted on showing me the proper technique in preparing C-Rations. He explained that there were three different cases of C-Rations, each case was marked either, B-1, B-2 or B-3. B-1 had things like Beef Steak, Ham Slices, Fruit, and

Crackers and Peanut Butter. B-2 had Beans and Wieners, Beefsteak with Potatoes, Ham and Lima Beans, Cheese Spread, Pecan Roll, and Pound Cake. B-3 cases contained Boned Chicken, Spiced Beef, Chicken and Noodles, and Bread and Jam. The accessory packs had plastic spoons, salt, pepper, coffee, sugar, creamer, Chiclets chewing gum and cigarettes.

Cleve said, "Joe, we treat all new guys to the best meal in all the boxes...Ham and Lima Beans, or better known as "Ham and Mother Fuckers!" The rest of the crew just smiled and nodded in agreement. Something inside me said I was being setup for a fall. Cleve then took out of his pocket a tiny metal can opener called a P-38. It's a very small piece of metal with a fold-out sharpened claw used to open the cans. He announced that the P-38 got its name because it takes 38 punctures to open a can. He then grabbed an old, used short C-Ration can, which already had the top cut off, and told me he was going to make me an official "John Wayne Boonie Stove." I watched, hoping to learn from these seasoned troops, how to properly prepare and cook these meals in a can. With his P-38, Cleve cut a couple of grooves in the can and pressed the sides in. This would hold up the can you were going to cook and let air in for the compressed Sterno tablet used to heat your meal. Next, he took another empty soup-sized can and told me to wash it out because this was going to be my drinking cup. He took a small piece of wood about four inches long and carved it round like a dowel. At each end he cut a groove. He then wrapped the top and bottom edges of the can with a piece of stiff wire, attaching the dowel. After several twists and turns around the can and dowel, he smiled and presented me with my first "jungle cup." I stared at it in amazement. Instead of using the Sterno heat tab, Cleve grabbed a block of C-4 plastic explosive and ripped off a small piece. He rolled it into a ball, placed it in the can and proceeded to light it. I ran out of the bunker as he struck the match. I thought he went crazy and was going to blow us all up. They all followed me out of the bunker, laughing and screaming at me as I ran and took cover, waiting for the big explosion. Finally, after they stopped laughing, they explained how C-4 will only burn when lit, will only explode with a detonator, and is used all the time for cooking. I still thought they had all gone a little nutty. To their surprise, I enjoyed the "Ham and Mothers". I quickly learned that "Beanie Weenies" was the number one meal on the DMZ. They became my favorite, but I would have to wait my turn for this meal.

The following morning, my training consisted of driving around the camp three times and becoming rear security on my first convoy, heading to a place called the "The Rockpile". On the way to our destination, we had to cross a river at a place called the Khe Gio Bridge. I still remember Calya yelling instructions, "Keep up the RPMs! Don't go too fast into the water! Stay to the left!" "There's a big concrete block under the water from the old bridge. Stay to the left!" I was more than a little nervous and did all the wrong things, including hitting the concrete block. That was all I remembered. The Driver's hatch, weighing about 100 lbs., slammed closed on top of me, forcing the periscope mount through my plastic Driver's helmet and knocking me out cold. They told me I slid down on top of the gas pedal and the track went out of control. It went down the river, up and over several embankments and into the elephant grass before they finally got me off the controls. While this was happening, the convoy was being shot at by some NVA and we weren't shooting back. I was thankful no one was hurt or killed. A few days later, we were told all hatches had to be tied open. Darryl Hale would always remind everyone how I almost got him killed on that convoy.

I learned there was a great responsibility in being the Driver. In our three-day training period, we were taught only the basic Driver duties: keep the Duster gassed, greased, oiled, and full of ammunition, ready to travel. I thought if there was any chance of going home or getting the crew in the turret home, I'd better learn all I could about this hunk of steel called a "DUSTER." I started asking questions, lots of questions. I asked about "**INCOMING!**," outgoing, past battles, land mines, Marines, jets, helicopters, medivacs, Army units, first aid, call signs, radio frequencies, convoys, convoy ambush deployment, grid coordinates, and the names of the radio operators from Dong Ha to Khe Sanh. I was shocked how we all learned from my questioning.

As I became a proper, gung-ho Duster Driver, I gave my Duster its own insignia. On the front turret plate above the 40mm cannon barrels, I painted a white skull with the words "GRIM REAPER."

I began ending all radio calls with my track number, followed by "Grim Reaper." I wanted everybody to know who we were and where we were, always. This wasn't radio protocol, but I didn't care who got offended. It was my butt on the line and, when I needed assistance, I could cut out the protocol bullshit and get down to business. The camp's "Office Pogues", shooting from the hip, tried to tell us what was happening on the road. The Duster Crews were the Road Warriors. We knew what was happening on Route 9 and we didn't need some asshole up on the hill telling us what to do. We called ourselves "The Thundering Herd".

I was proud to be the Driver. It taught me the meaning of true teamwork, the value of courage under fire, the commitment you must be willing to give to another human being, and what it meant when they said, "There are those who just drive and there are those who are drivers." You knew when you achieved true Driver status. The crew from the turret would start telling jokes about you. The best joke was, "My Driver's so stupid that, during a fire fight, he will open the front door of the track, get out from the safety of the Driver's compartment, and tap dance around the outside of the Duster, while handing us ammo in tune to the rhythm of the enemy's AK-47s." Jokes about anyone or anything seemed to break the cutting edge of war.

The troops in our part of the war zone often said, "If Hell could be renamed, it would be called Route 9, the Road to Khe Sanh." Route 9 or "THE ROAD", as we called it, was to become my home, my way of life. It was as if only our Duster knew the way to all the other camps. Our track would run the road an average of five to six days per week. If it wasn't what we called "regular convoys", it was a small convoy the Marines called "The Rough Rider". Sometimes we would do area sweeps with the Marines, search and destroy missions or body recovery.

I remember the first time an "RPG" (Rocket Propelled Grenade) was fired at our track. It was my third or fourth convoy to The Rockpile. I was about a half-mile past the Khe Gio Bridge. All of a sudden, an NVA soldier jumped out of the elephant grass, brought a tube-like object to his shoulder, shot, and jumped back in the grass just as fast. Like a giant smoking bottle rocket, it flew at us like a vision from an old Flash Gordon flick, spitting smoke and flying sporadically with the Gook acting the part of Ming the Merciless. The RPG hit the ground in front of us, exploded and sent hot metal and dirt all over us. Like some crazy man, I drove into the tall grass, hoping to run over the little Gook bastard. I was instantly ordered to a slow crawl, and we started shooting into the tall grass. We allowed the first three vehicles in the convoy to pass us. The firefight ended as fast as it started.

When we got to The Rockpile, the only conversation about the incident was among our own crew. They laughed that the Gook had missed us by a mile. If that was a mile, I'd hate to see what they considered close. I guess laughing built courage. We replenished our ammo and took another convoy back to Camp Carroll. I always wondered if I had run over that NVA soldier. The guys in the turret said I got him, but I didn't think so. I thought I should have felt a thump or something as I ran him over. Maybe when twenty-five tons of steel going 40mph runs over someone, you don't feel too much. When we got back to camp, I asked if we were supposed to file an incident report or notify the Captain. I was shocked when I was told that no one cared. We only report the seriously wounded or the dead. They didn't ask and we didn't tell. The only time they cared was if a lifer sergeant or officer riding with us got hurt. We'd then tell them all about the battle. They'd get their medals and maybe we'd get some recognition. Purple Hearts were a dime a dozen and, unless you were really bleeding and needed a medic, we didn't bother reporting injuries. I would soon learn that my first Squad Leader was telling the sad truth. There were only four ways you left our outfit: dead, missing some parts, missing in action, or your tour was over. Army soldiers attached to the Marines had their rules, and I quickly learned what rules kept me alive and what rules would get me killed.

"Duster"
M42   Twin 40-mm Cannons, Self Propelled – Automatic Weapon
Front View

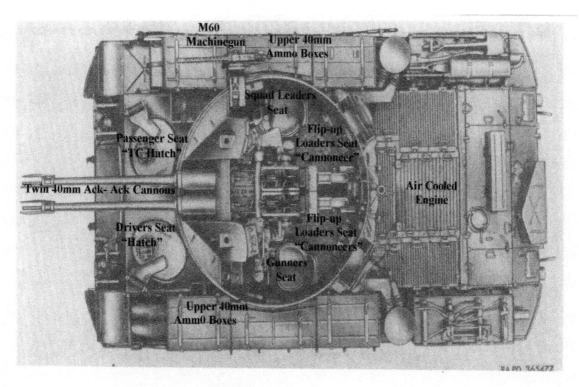

"Duster"
Top View

Duster – Twin 40mm breaches loaded for action.

Standing on my Duster holding a clip of 40mm ammunition.

Manning my Duster's M-60 machine gun.

Claymore Mine

The training sergeant said that anything seen in these sights must "Die."

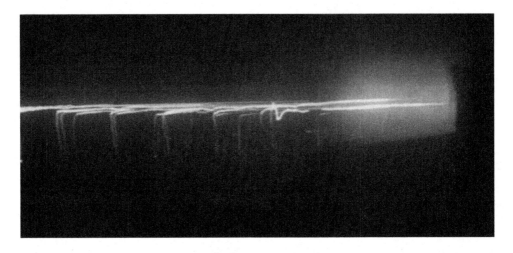

Duster 40mm shooting at night.

Quad 50 machine guns mounted on 21/2 ton trucks.
Note: The nose art on the front shield of the right truck -
"The Widow Maker" was the most famous Quad 50.

Quad 50 machine guns with special cooling aircraft barrels.

Quad 50 shooting at night.

John "Tank" Huelsenbeck.

Loading the "Newbee's" on the 21/2 ton truck at Dong Ha.

*Passing the Vietnamese relocation settlement outside
Cam Lo called "Tin City" on Route 9.*

Montagnard Village relocated next to "Tin City."

Charlie Battery main area at Camp Carroll.

*Dave Woods standing next to Charlie Battery sign at
Camp J.J. Carroll.*

*Lieutenant Steve Moore
Lt. Mitchum can be seen in the background wearing a baseball cap.*

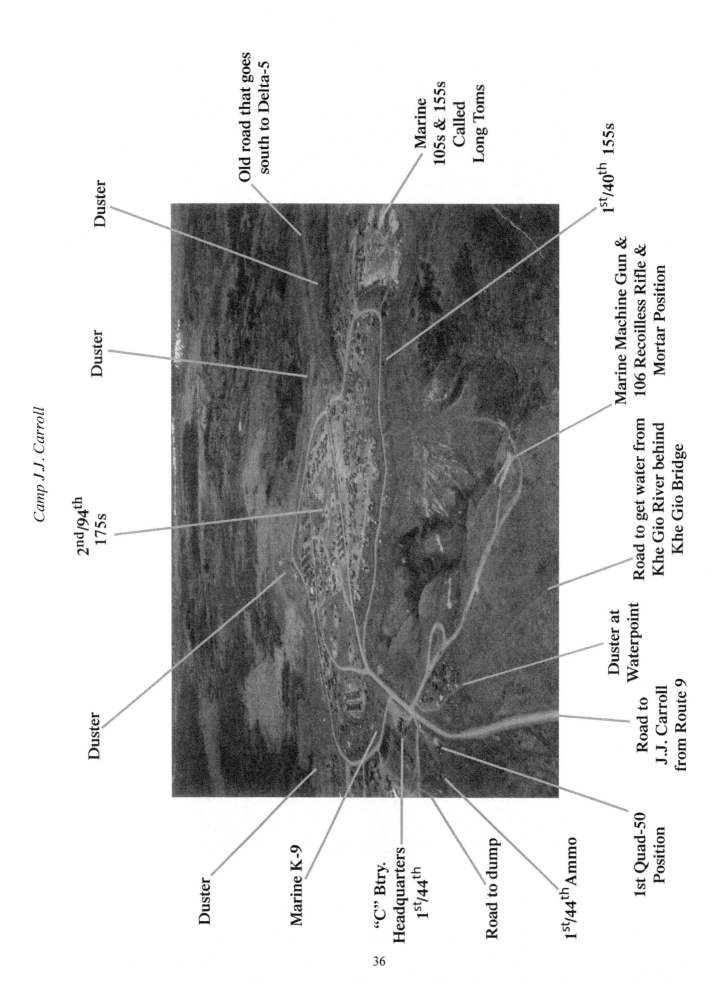

Camp J.J. Carroll

Camp Carroll looking from the South to the North.
Note: The Lookout Tower next to the Waterpoint position in the distance.
Headquarters of Charlie Battery, 1/44 Artillery, is to the right of the Tower.

Duster motor pool at Camp Carroll.

I painted my new call new sign and symbol "Grim Reaper" on our Duster.

Grim Reaper Duster at Camp Carroll waterpoint position.

The Driver's seat of my Duster.
The 40mm ammo cans are stored beside the Driver.

2nd/94th Artillery – 175mm Cannon.

Charlie Battery – "The Thundering Herd."

Convoy assembling to travel down Route 9.

The original Khe Gio Bridge lying in the water,
the place where I hit the old concrete piers.

Chapter 3: LOST INNOCENCE

September 6, 1967: I received a small pocket diary from my brother-in-law, Kenny. I now have a place for my thoughts. ***That little book and some treasured scraps of paper would be the safe keepers of my year in Nam.*** If I die, my family will have some knowledge of what I had experienced.

Dear Diary,

BUNKER DREAMS

Uncurling from my fetal position of sleep, I realized I was not alone. To my surprise and pleasure, my mind had brought me a Monk to see me through the night. As he stood there hidden by his majestic raven cloak, I was shamefully reminded of Bela Lugosi. I accepted him wholeheartedly, although he was featureless, except for the outline of a painfully thin person. This apparition waited patiently and finally spoke. The voice, though not lucid, was calm and warm, trained on a thousand rosaries. I sat up, waiting to be filled with his words of wisdom, like a balloon readying itself for a helium trip. I was in the confessional of life. "Please speak,"
I begged him, "I need your words to help me this night." My Monk just stood there, motionless in his stance of prayer. I stood to apologize for something I did not know. Finally, I comprehended why my Monk had arrived. Protruding from beneath his cloak was the skinless bones of a foot and the blade of his Reaper's Scythe swishing through the air screaming... "INCOMING!"

September 7: We were called out as part of a reactionary force to find a missing Marine lost in this morning's firefight. We searched the ambush area with a small squad of Marines. After about an hour of driving through the elephant grass, we found him. He had been tortured by the NVA. His back was broken and his pecker stuffed in his mouth. We all cried and swore our vengeance. I never knew his name, ***may God forgive me***. We could only pray for his soul and hope someone knew his name. ***Dear God, please don't let that happen to me.*** My innocence was being destroyed before my eyes. I prayed to what I hoped were not deaf ears.

Dear God, I have only been here a few short weeks. There is so much death, especially the enemy. Please make me strong for what I have to do. This isn't football, track, or boxing. Make me quick with no hesitations. I know my job is to kill. I just never knew I would be good at it. I'm afraid this war will make me another type of person, someone my family won't like. God, maybe it's the Duster that makes us kill. We keep her well fed on a diet of NVA. I don't know how to explain it to you, God. I am already caught up in her rhythm of killing. ***Forgive me…***

September 8: I met my first Marine Gunnery Sergeant. They just call him "Gunny". His men adore him. He is like their Messiah. We sat around joking and getting to know each other. The Marines called me a "doggy" soldier and taunted me, saying that Army meant, **"Ain't Ready to be a Marine Yet."** We all laughed and I teased them about being called "Jar Heads". I thought they were from a Marine unit called 1/9 and nicknamed "The Walking Dead". The Gunny was telling all of us how he wished Chesty Puller was here. Chesty would do things right, Chesty would do this, and Chesty would do that. I chirped in and announced. "If Chesty were here, I'd do her right, too." With that announcement, the Gunny attacked me as if I had said something bad about his mother. To his and the other Marines' surprise, I quickly knocked him on his ass several times and almost knocked him out. After all the commotion, they told me Chesty Puller was the most famous Marine that ever lived. I apologized to my Marine friends. I hadn't meant to insult them or Mr. Puller. I had no idea who he was or that he was the greatest Marine alive. The Marines nicknamed me "The General," a reference to when I disrespected their most beloved General.

Years later one midnight, I would meet Chesty's son, Lewis Puller, Jr., at The Wall (Vietnam Memorial) in Washington, D.C. I told him the story about his father and we laughed. I casually pushed him in his wheelchair along the Wall. Lewis had been seriously wounded in Nam and his wheelchair was now his chariot. It was as if we were the only two men there. We talked easily about our experiences and introduced each other to our friends on The Wall. We had a simple friendship that only lasted a few short years. I still listen to the audio version of his book, "Fortunate Son". Lewis, you are deeply missed.

September 9: I finally began to realize that we had a daily routine. The average day started at dusk. Each night, four of the five-man crew pulled two-hour shifts of Guard Duty. Daily, one man got a turn to get some extra sleep. Our Duster shot all night H&I missions. About an hour before sunup, we would leave camp with a small group of Marines. The morning ritual was called "mine sweeping". Marines walked in front of us with metal detectors. We swept about two miles of the road for landmines. We found them every day and the Marines blew them up in place. I felt sorry for the Grunt whose job it was to use the metal detector. It was sadistically comical when he found a landmine. He stopped real quick, waved his "magic wand" back and forth, and tapped several times on his headset as if confirming his newfound treasure. He stepped back and did it all again, and then waved for help. His teammates joked and told him he was on his own, and then they'd all curse out the landmine and each other...***building courage.*** They blew up the mines they found, and we'd all go back to camp and eat something. Hopefully, we could get a hot meal from one of the mess halls. If not, we ate C-Rations. We would then announce the famous military term "Saddle Up!" and leave the camp on some kind of other mission, either convoys, search and destroys, body recovery or extracting Marines from some isolated area, or hopefully just staying at camp.

September 10: Camp J.J. Carroll was hit by twenty NVA artillery shells. The sound of the shells screaming through the air made my brain cry out in fear. My heart nearly burst out of my chest and my bones ached as the shells exploded all around us. The ground shook and there was a horrible dusty, burnt smell as the bombs exploded and all I could hear was the shrapnel ripping things, and people, apart. The screaming of the wounded and dying could be heard over the explosions. All I could think of was being hit by one of those shells and my body ending up in thousands of tiny pieces splattered all over the DMZ. Nothing left of me to send home to my family. I don't know if I can ever get used to **"INCOMING!".**

Dear Heavenly Father, How can I explain to you what incoming and body recovery is doing to me, my brain, my heart, my body, my soul... my belief in you is changing. Please do not forsake me. If nothing else changes me in this war, this will...

My tour is now only into its second week, and I am in the Duster doing what we call "the mail run" to Dong Ha and back to Camp Carroll. On the return trip, we were advised by radio to go up the road that led to a place called Con Thien. We were to act as a reactionary force for some Marine tanks hit by the NVA on the road that left Con Thien to Route 9. This was to be my christening into what the Grunts or Infantry called "COMBAT." For some strange reason, I thought I had already experienced combat. Maybe someone forgot to inform me. We didn't travel very far before we saw a tank and some trucks stationary on the road about a hundred or more yards in front of us. It looked like they were on fire. Shooting could be heard everywhere. I was told to stop the Duster. The Squad Leader spoke briefly to someone on the radio. I was sweating and holding tight to the steering bar. Within seconds, the Twin 40s started shooting. The noise of the 40s shooting over my head is always a new experience. Each shell fired hurt my ears and made me twitch in my seat. I was ordered to proceed at a crawl toward the smoking tank and to stop no closer than a hundred feet from it.

As we approached the tank, I could see smoke coming out of the top hatch and engine compartment. Two men, who I thought were tank crew, were lying on the outside of the tank. Behind it I could see a few trucks in the trench alongside the road. About a dozen Marines were scattered along the road. Three or four were still shooting, the others were not moving. It was a horrible scene. Then the order came, but not the one I was waiting for. I was hoping we were going to leave. It was the order I would learn to hate the most, "Ammo up!" It meant my guys in the turret were almost out of ammunition. If we stopped shooting, we could die. Frantically, I started to open the reserve 40mm ammunition stored in the Driver's compartment. Each ammo can weighed 116 pounds and held 16 shells. As fast as I could hand out ammo was as fast as they shot it. Soon, there was no room to move in the Driver's compartment because I never threw out the empty ammo cans or lids. I realized, for the first time, I had to open the front door of the Duster and get out. Bullets were pinging off the Duster hull like a drum roll. I took what I hoped was not my last deep breath, kicking open the front door and jumping out of the Duster.

Not knowing what to do with the empty cans, I somewhat hastily stacked them next to the Duster as I handed ammo up to the men in the turret. My back was to the enemy. I continually turned around and gave short bursts with my M-16 in the direction the enemy bullets were coming from. Like some kind of wild tap dancer, I followed the back of the turret as it traversed, handing ammo up to the Cannoneers. Above all the noise, I could hear someone yelling for help. I saw a Marine trying to crawl to the safety of our Duster. He was covered in blood and yet was trying to drag a fellow wounded Marine with him. All he wanted me to do was save his friend. I don't know why, but I ran to him. Grabbing his friend and flipping him up onto my left shoulder, fireman's style, I ran back to the Duster, placing him inside my Driver's compartment. As I ran, his blood covered my hands, arms, shoulder and neck. As he bounced on my shoulder, I could feel his warm blood pumping into my ear and running down my back and chest. It made me tremble. Before I knew it, I had four Marines piled inside the Driver's compartment next to my seat, packed so tightly I had trouble closing the door. The Squad Leader was screaming at me to get back in the Duster. He had me "neutral steer" 180 degrees around and told me to "Dee Dee-Move Fast" and drive as fast as I could back towards Route 9 until he told me to stop. As I drove, the minutes seemed like hours. I didn't know what was happening. I could no longer see all the action. I just sat there, holding the steering bar tight, trembling with fear. The Squad Leader chirped into my headset to stop. I could not help but stare at the wounded Marines piled next to me in my small Driver's compartment, moaning and asking for help. The loud bursts of the shooting 40s reawakened me to the reality of war. Over the intercom, I could hear the Squad Leader screaming at the men in the turret. Patiently, I waited for my next order. Again, the thought of really dying entered my mind. ***Who would tell my parents?*** All at once the shooting stopped.

Reinforcements must have come out from Con Thien or another base, because Marines were all over the place and seemed to be assessing the damage. I advised the Squad Leader that we had four wounded Marines stacked in the Driver's compartment. He started yelling at me and then said something inaudible into the radio. He said "Dee Dee" and we quickly left the ambush site and went to a place called the Cam Lo Compound. We left the wounded at a small medivac station. I was mentally shook up and totally lost and had to be directed back to camp. Two were injured badly. The guy who was crawling had a hole in his face and one through his leg. The fourth guy, I think, was dead. He never moved or said anything. I had no idea what to do for them and feel guilty that I may not have done the right things in my first firefight.

After we got back at Camp Carroll, the crew was very quiet and stayed to themselves. I began to clean the blood out of the Driver's hatch area. I cried as I cleaned, hoping that the crew would not notice. I had to suck up all my emotions if I was to be accepted. Soldiers don't cry. I thought, 'God, we're with the Marines. I've got to suck it up.' I was surprised that the whole incident had taken less than three hours from start to finish. I cleaned up all the blood and was starting to fill the inside of the Duster with new ammo. One of the Cannoneers came out and told me that the Sarge wanted to see me in the bunker. I was shocked at how angry he was with me. He told me to never pick up the wounded or the dead until all the shooting stopped—not even the Duster personnel. My main objective was to keep the track running, help with ammo, shoot my M-16, help with the radio, and make damn sure no Gooks got on or close to the Duster. Dusters are killing machines and it is our job to protect the Grunts and kill the enemy before he kills our troops or us. The Driver is the most important crewmember. If he didn't do his job, nobody went home. I was determined to be able to do both jobs, keep the crew safe and supplied with ammo, and pick up the wounded and dead.

The Sarge then started yelling at everyone. We all cleaned the Duster and got it ready for the next convoy. After we were finished, he told me I had to burn my fatigue shirt because it was covered in someone else's blood and it was bad luck to keep the shirt. I knew I needed all the luck I could get and didn't argue. I dipped the shirt in the diesel fuel and gas mixture we used to clean our 40mm cannons. In silent tribute to another human's essence, I lit the shirt on fire. The Sarge nodded in satisfaction. Again, there was no official acknowledgement of the day's firefight. At the mess hall that evening, a few of us briefly went over the battle with the men from the camp. My fellow soldiers always wanted to know all about the blood and guts of the firefights. Lt. Moore walked by and told us what a good job we had done. His words of praise were mixed with words of Christianity. We were shocked he even knew of the battle. I should have known better; he was the best officer we had.

Dear Lord, I don't know if I can live up to the Sergeant's rules about not helping the wounded and dying during a battle. Something inside me says I cannot let any of them down. Maybe if I learn more and practice more, I can fight and save lives at the same time. Help me, Lord, this war will test my mettle.

September 11: Between all the convoys we run up and down Route 9, we have to make mail runs all alone to Dong Ha and back to Camp Carroll. Sometimes we bring a small convoy back with us. We notice on each trip back that there are always the same three Vietnamese people standing at the end of the Cam Lo Village, two men and a woman. One of the men holds a pen and clipboard and starts writing as we pass. When we get about a mile down the road, we always get hit by the NVA. We agree that, by the way they are dressed, they are brazen NVA soldiers and are sending convoy info to their comrades. The days they are not there we don't get hit. They are so bold that I was able to take a picture of them. ***Bastards!***

September 12: Besides being a target for every NVA artillery unit, camp life has other kinds of obstacles. My friend, Rodriguez, came to my position on the perimeter of the camp and told me the Sergeant sent him to fetch me for shit burning and piss tube detail. I started laughing, thinking he was joking. "It's your turn. You've been pissing in the tubes and taking a dump in the main camp's shitter for weeks. Now you can clean and burn." "Thanks a lot, buddy." The latrine, or shithouse, is a small wooden structure. Inside there are two wooden planks with four holes cut into each plank for you to sit on and have your moment of peace and comfort. There are no toilet seats, just wood splinters from the rough-cut holes. The only problem is that you can be sitting with seven other guys, knees touching, wanting the same experience and begging for toilet paper. Toilet paper is a prized commodity.

The first thing he showed me was where the lime and window screening were stored. After loading a wheelbarrow with lime and grabbing a handful of window screens, that were pre-cut to about two-foot squares, we started off for my new adventure, "Shit Burning Detail." The first thing we walked to was one of the piss tubes. The tubes were the empty storage cylinders from Howitzer cannon shells. A hole was dug into the ground and the tube was placed at a forty-five degree angle, crotch high. The window screen was wrapped around the open end for you to pee through. The screen also prevented jungle critters from getting in the tube and biting your pecker. He explained that if the screens had holes, I was to replace them. Then I was to throw lime all around the piss tube area. There were six piss tubes spread around Charlie Battery's main area and only one main, eight-seat shitter. Next I was to pull the eight cut-in-half 50 gallon drums full of rank shit and piss out of the back of the outhouse. I was to fill them with kerosene, add a little gasoline, roll up some newspaper, light it, and toss it into the drum. While the shit burned, and between stirrings, I was to finish working on the piss tubes. Rodriguez walked away laughing and yelled, "Have fun and don't get killed!" With the flick of my Zippo lighter, I lit a piece of rolled up paper and tossed it in the can. Instantly, flames started licking at the shit, with lots of billowing black, smelly smoke. In a flash all the cans were lit and on fire, a towering black inferno full of the nastiest smells on earth. I stirred each can with a long stick as if I were stirring a pot of my favorite soup. It was an easy job. All I had to do was stand there and occasionally stir the brew until it turned to ashes. There was only one problem. It took more than four hours to burn an eight-can shitter. I was covered in what they called "shit ash," plus the smoke was a giant target for all the NVA artillery teams in the area. Burn, stir, and dodge artillery. It was lots of "fun".

I always wondered if I was to get killed while burning shit, would my parents get a letter saying "Your son died while burning human waste" or maybe "in the line of "doodie".

<u>September 14:</u> I was curious about the August 21st battle and the men we replaced because of it. Lt. Moore, John Huelsenbeck and Don Wolfe went into great detail telling me that Charlie Battery was part of Captain John Ripley's Raiders, Lima Company, 3rd Battalion – 3rd Marines, and that, on the 21st , they were involved in another big battle on Route 9.

A super convoy, about a mile long, was traveling from The Rockpile to Ca Lu and got hit halfway to Ca Lu. Reactionary forces from the Rockpile and Ca Lu went to the rescue. Lt. Steve Moore came from Ca Lu commanding two Dusters. With him were Eugene Triola and Joseph Musso. As they approached the ambush, the NVA turned several RPGs in their direction, hitting the Marine M48 Tank in front of them and knocking it out of commission. Moore's two Dusters then started shooting full auto at the rushing NVA infantry. RPGs were flying overhead and exploding all around them. On full auto, they quickly exhausted the 40mm ammo in the turret boxes. As the Driver opened the reserved stored ammunition from inside the Duster hull, Moore ran around the sides of the Duster and tossed them up to the Cannoneers in the turret. Seeing the enemy's .51 caliber machine gun shooting at the piper cub spotter plane, he directed his Duster to take out the enemy's gun. The pilot chirped on the radio a big "Thank You." Two NVA then physically attacked Moore. He shot one with his .45 pistol and dispatched the other in a hand-to-hand battle. One of the

NVA slightly wounded him with a bayonet during their brief struggle. As they advanced forward, enemy mortars exploded all around them, wounding Moore and his crew with splinters of hot shrapnel. Slowly, they fought their way east into the ambushed convoy, knocking out any NVA positions they encountered.

Two Dusters and one 2 ½ truck full of 40mm ammunition advanced towards the ambush from The Rockpile. The two Duster crews were comprised of Lt. Stephen Drennen and Dustermen Sgt. Dailey, Ed Hoffman, Cooper Thomas, Don Wolfe, Joseph Konopka, Buddy Russell, Billy Watson, Roger Lewis, Juan Valenzuela, Larry Wiegert, and Duster Driver Donald Gerber.

Leaving The Rockpile, they proceeded at full speed toward the ambush. Riding on top of their Duster was a squad of Marines and Captain John Ripley, holding tight to the turret and the M60 machine gun. Before they could even approach the destroyed convoy, a second NVA unit, waiting in hiding, sprung a full scale "L-Shaped" surprise attack. Volleys of NVA RPGs began shooting from both sides of the road, flying inches over the top of the Duster. A few of the RPGs hit the ground in front of their moving Dusters and ammo truck. The combat-experienced Drivers accelerated through the maze of explosions which covered them and their crews in red hot metal and smoldering earth. The bullets were so fierce that they shot the tip off of Joe Konopka's M-16 and put a hole through the rifle stock. Captain Ripley instantly grabbed the Duster's M60 machine gun, positioned next to Don Wolfe, and opened up at the rushing NVA, unloading two full cans of ammo on them. As the next volley of RPGs flew over Ripley's head, he turned to Don and his Marines and yelled, "We're getting off this fucking metal coffin. These guys are crazy!" Like human torpedoes, they all dove off the moving Duster into the tall elephant grass and charged the enemy on foot.

John Huelsenbeck, with Steve Williams, drove a 2 ½ ton truck full of ammunition and was positioned between the two Dusters. As their truck rolled forward, one of the enemy mortars landed between him and the Duster, ripping holes in the truck fenders and hood. Next, the truck windows were blown out and the right side of the truck was riddled by NVA heavy machine gun fire. John, grabbing his M-16 and his Marine grenade bag, bailed out of the moving truck, followed by Williams. Forced to leave the truck, they took cover in an old bomb crater. Hearing NVA talking and shouting, they started to fight their way up the sides of the road, killing any NVA in their path. The second Duster, unable to advance forward, pushed the destroyed ammo truck off the road.

Because of the physical strength of the NVA, it was very difficult to advance forward or backward. To protect their left flank, Sgt. Dailey's Duster positioned itself, alone, in an open flat space of land between the road and the rushing enemy. As both Dusters and Marine combat teams fought off the NVA, John Huelsenbeck noticed Juan Valenzuela slumped over the turret. Quickly, he climbed on top of the Duster and realized Juan had been killed. Placing Juan on the back of the Duster, John started helping load the 40mm cannons and got the Duster shooting again. Dailey's Duster called for more ammo. They were out and being overrun. Steve Williams called John Huelsenbeck and advised him of Dailey's situation. Huelsenbeck and Williams, assigned as the only ammo team for the firefight, grabbed two cans of ammo and ran to their aid. Lt. Drennen ordered John and Steve to go get more ammo. Before they could return, the NVA hit Drennen's Duster with an RPG. The RPG penetrated the Duster turret, fatally wounding Watson, Lewis and Wiegert. Hundreds strong, the NVA then boarded the Duster and shot the men a second time, guaranteeing their kills. Lt. Drennen, now shot through the jaw, escaped being killed by diving head first into the TC hatch.

Don Wolfe's Duster crew, having witnessed their friends being killed, instantly turned their guns on the NVA and killed them. John and Steve, shocked, looked on in disbelief. Billy Watson had been one of John's best friends.

During the entire battle, other Dusterman were trapped on trucks in the center of the ambush. Lindsay Baldoni and Leroy Gerber were killed by the first wave of NVA. Joe Murphy on a Duster fuel truck, along with other Dusterman, fought off the NVA with their M-16 and prayed the truck would not explode and go up in flames. The remaining Dustermen would always thank the Marines for coming to their rescue.

The battle lasted all day and took several days to clean up. After the battle, they loaded their dead and wounded comrades on the back of their Duster and ammo truck and limped back to The Rockpile. Lt. Steve Moore was awarded the Bronze Star with "V" Device. Don Wolfe and John Huelsenbeck were each awarded the Army Commendation Metal for their heroism.

Marine, Leonard Bud, was taken prisoner.

He was held as a Prisoner of War and was not released until 1973.

They then told stories of other similar enemy battles, one on April 25th when Joshua Atkins, Leonard Thomas, and Joseph Royster were killed and another on May 7th when Rhoden Talmadge, Franklin Lewis and Thomas Evans got killed. I was horrified as they told their stories.

They explained to me that nobody really ever talked about the battles or their friends killed in action. They each spoke of an inner hurt and tried to explain that you are given no time to grieve, no day off, and there is no way you can tell their family how you cared. Plus, there was no funeral for you to attend. You just went on as if nothing had ever happened, as though your friends never existed. They then went on to say that I should expect the same scenario during my tour with the 44th.

September 16: We did another mail run today to Dong Ha. I was the lead Duster on our trip back, followed by three supply trucks. As we got to the Cam Lo area, I slowed the Duster down hoping to find and see our three NVA friends. Like clockwork we could see them standing in their same spot. This time we were ready for them. As we approached them, I shot and killed the guy with the clipboard. The other guy and girl quickly ran and disappeared into the bushes. The guys in the turret opened up on them with their M-16s. We think we got them because we did not get a hit today.

September 17: I received a package from Rome. It was from my Uncle Nick's sister. She was a nun named Sister Mercedes who was stationed at the Vatican and was an emissary to Pope Paul VI. Inside the package were five sets of rosary beads and a dozen small medallions with the picture of the Pope and a letter. The only problem was that the letter was written in either Italian or Latin. Knowing she was multi-lingual, I copied her address and wrote her a letter.

Each month I received a letter from her written in English, along with a few rosary beads and other tokens blessed by the Pope. Regardless of religious belief, the guys cherished the blessed gifts from the Pontiff.

September 21: The NVA blew up the Dong Ha ammunition depot. What an explosion, it could be seen for miles.

September 22: Vietnam is the most beautiful place I have ever seen. Where I live in the north is very mountainous and the vegetation grows tall and green. The mountains are like razor sharp spears sticking out of the earth, looming over giant rolling lush green hills. The dirt is reddish in color. In our area, we have old pineapple, banana, coffee, and tapioca plantations, which were once owned by the French and American produce companies. Every day I see giant wild boars running across the road, and monkeys and mongoose. Occasionally, I see some sort of very tiny deer, no more than two feet tall. Insects are gigantic. There are scorpions and spiders of all sizes and shapes. We have eight-inch long centipedes, green and orange in color with half-inch pinchers. I see all kinds of snakes. The ones I worry about were the Cobras and a snake they call a "Green Bamboo Viper," or the "Step-and-a-Half Snake," because that's all you will take before you drop dead. Before you take a dump in the latrines or the makeshift toilets the Marines call a "Head", you have to stick your head down in the shitter and look under the piece of wood your butt is about to sit on to check and see what assortment of creatures are waiting to bite your ass.

While digging one of our fighting holes the other day, we uncovered a very large worm about sixteen inches long. We first thought it was a snake, but one of the guys told us it was just a worm. Leeches stick to us like glue and roaches crawl inside our clothes. Rats seem to be the biggest everyday problem while at camp. They constantly crawl on us in our sleep or over our feet while we write letters home. I'm not talking your average size rat, but a rat that's about as big as a rabbit.

September 23: We were assigned a new position guarding the main entrance to Camp Carroll and the western and northern slopes. They call it "The Water Point Position" because all the purified drinking water for the combat bases in the area is made there. Plus, it is the closest Duster position to the main gate for taking out the daily convoys and doing other crazy Marine missions. I don't like how this position is situated. It is away from the main camp and we are sitting at the tip of a long finger, making us an easy three-sided target for the enemy.

September 24: Carroll was hit by 88 NVA rockets. The Rockpile was hit by 21 enemy rockets. We never have body bags and just use ponchos, poncho liners, or pieces of tent to wrap the dead. It is sad that, as the Body Recovery Team, we don't have body bags. Recovery is a job from the bowels of Hell. We drop off the wounded at the medical or medivac areas. The dead are taken to a makeshift location called "Graves Registration". I have become too acquainted with Graves Registration. I taste the stench and smell of death. My insides never stop crying. ***Is this what my Dad experienced in WWII? Suck it up, Joe, suck it up!***

Every time we are at camp, I practice getting ammo out from the Driver's compartment. Never again am I going to let down anyone in my crew or on the battlefield. I learn how to load the 40s, clean the 40s, unjam the 40s, shoot the 40s, call in fire missions, and am determined that everyone on the crew know each other's job. If one of us gets hurt, the others will take up the slack. I asked the medic for a crash safety course and extra medical supplies.

Eventually, I would demand from my fellow crewmembers their whole-hearted effort in learning everything they could about the Duster. I would hold training classes and, if necessary, become physical to prove my conviction to teamwork and effort. Don Wolfe told me I had a reputation as a badass city kid and that was okay with me. I beat a few asses and thus they all knew I meant business. "Let the training begin," said I.

September 25: At 19:30 hours we were on the receiving end of about 30 NVA artillery shells. Ninety minutes later, we were barraged again by 30 more NVA shells. Diving for cover became a new Olympic sport.

Today we went to the Camp Carroll Mess Hall and we were harassed by one of the Marines. This is not the first time we have had trouble with this particular Marine. He likes to pick on the new guys and spit in their food or stir it with his finger. Yelling that he is trying to make us Army Dogs tough like Marines, I instantly hate this guy and want to punch his lights out. But I am told to "cool it" and to "chill out".

September 26: We luck out and are sent for a week to "Hill 250" just outside Camp Carroll. My new crew consists of Squad Leader Eugene Triola, Gunner Johnny Towns, and Cannoneers James Biers and Dwayne King. I am the Driver. Triola gave me my first .45 caliber pistol. It makes me feel good to have my own personal weapon. I am tired of borrowing one. He told me to just keep it out of sight. It is not considered regular issue equipment.

Hill 250 is possibly the best position on the DMZ. It is a hilltop outpost with a magnificent 360 degree view of the DMZ. On top of the hill is a Ground Surveillance Radar team who help locate the direction of enemy artillery. A platoon of Marines and a lookout tower gives us an even better view of the area. It is our job to shoot at any enemy movement, shoot any enemy artillery that is in our range, or give our big artillery shooting coordinates.

September 27: I could see, in the valley, a large group of what I thought were NVA crossing the Cam Lo River. The crew confirmed my sightings. I was so nervous giving the 105mm Artillery Unit's FDC (Fire Direction Center) the grid coordinates of their location. Each crewmember confirmed my map grids. I didn't want to be alone in my uncertain decision. I prayed that God would forgive me for killing. Our training seemed to make the enemy less than human and okay to kill. We followed the heavy artillery with a few hundred Duster 40mm rounds and saw some secondary explosions. Later in the afternoon, a Marine officer brought us a case of cold beer, a rare commodity on the DMZ, and congratulated us on a job well done. He drank a cold one with us, climbed onto the Duster, sat in the Gunner's seat, and made like he was shooting the Duster. He shouted, "You guys have to be fuckin' nuts to be in one of these metal coffin-RPG magnets!" He then saluted and left the hill. Our crew sat there drinking beer and praising our kills for the day.

Beer never seemed to taste the same again. A cold beer for taking a life. It's been over forty years and I still won't drink the stuff.

September 28: One of the guys going home gave me his battery-operated record player. It is great, complete with records and a couple dozen batteries. Along with listening to Gunsmoke on the radio, dancing around the bunker to Motown, country, and folk music gives me a taste of home. Now we will be able to listen to Hanoi Hannah spout her bullshit about killing Americans—asshole!

September 29: Tank and the other seasoned Dustermen finally started calling me by my real name. Billy Watson's soul can finally rest in peace.

September 30: We have very little contact with the native people. There seem to be two types of people in this area, the Vietnamese and the Montagnards or "Mountain People". The "Yards", as we call them, are an indigenous group of people, living a lifestyle that reminds me of the jungle natives of South America and Africa, complete with crossbows and blow guns. Their homes are made of thatch and straw. To promote harmony, peace, and trade, our unit has the Vietnamese people in the relocation settlement at Cam Lo do some of our laundry. We very seldom get back the same clothes we send.

My favorite activity is visiting and helping the Montagnards. The children are very pleasant and loved candy. I give them Bazooka Bubble Gum and teach them how to blow bubbles. After a few tries, they swallow the gum. They are very friendly to Americans and support the war effort against the NVA. It is easy to realize why they like us and not the NVA.

Airplanes spraying Agent Orange.
The troops could feel the oily mist sticking to them.

NVA soldiers, two men and a woman,
brazenly standing in NVA clothes, hiding under Cooley hats.

"Burning human waste,"
also known as "Shit burning detail"

The billowing black smoke from the burning shit made a
great target for enemy cannons, rockets, and mortars.

Aerial view of a Duster shooting.
In the turret, sitting in the Squad leader's seat is Don Wolfe
(no shirt). In the Gunner's seat is Cleve Lanier. Standing on the rear
deck are Cooper Thomas (white shirt) and Leslie "Red" Dietze.

Left to right: Cleve Lanier, Donald Wolfe, and Leslie "Red" Dietze.

Billy Watson and John "Tank" Huelsenbeck, best friends.
Billy was "Killed In Action" on August 21, 1967.

Left to right: John Gunesch, Noble Grinner, Wayne Bailey, 1st SGT
Boone, Steve Harris and Frank Bardone.

Marines mine sweeping Route 9.

Dong Ha ammunition depot blowing up.

New Jersey flag sent to me by Governor Hughes.

Montagnard Village past Ca Lu in the area called Joliet.
The woman pictured is thrashing rice on a bamboo mat. By the
look of the pile of old husks, she has been thrashing in the same area for years.

CHAPTER 4:
TO REALLY LIVE-YOU MUST NEARLY DIE

October 3: We were rear Security on a supply convoy headed for another outpost called Ca Lu. It was eerie how we drove through The Rockpile without stopping. We just yelled hellos and dirty slogans at the troops in the camp. This stretch of the road always made me very nervous. I was driving again into what we called "Ambush Alley – The Road to Hell". As if from nowhere, the trucks in the middle of the convoy were riddled by NVA automatic weapons. Bombs exploded everywhere. Marines jumping out of their trucks were being disembodied by small NVA anti-personnel mines. It happened so fast, I was almost against the bumper of the truck in front of me. I quickly backed up the Duster a good 100 feet and stopped along the right shoulder of the road. Before I finished backing up, the Duster started shooting. Each burst of the 40s' high explosive rounds shredded the elephant grass, trees, and leaves, ripping the enemy to pieces. Debris and human parts were flying everywhere. It was our time to kill. The guys called it "Mowing Grass."

We advanced ever so slowly, shooting in close to the convoy. Then shooting a few hundred yards away, we made our mark of death on Mother Earth in the shape of a giant square with an "X" in the middle. Again, "Joe! Ammo! Ammo! Ammo up!" was screamed into my headset. By now, after several firefights, I was prepared to leave the sanctuary of my Driver's compartment and hand up more ammo to the turret. In the Driver's compartment, I had started carrying a few empty .50 caliber ammunition cans full of hand grenades. Before I exited the hatch, I threw one grenade to the left and one to the right, to hopefully kill any Gooks who had gotten close to my Duster. Then, I jumped out of the track onto the ground and fired a quick burst from my M-16 into the same areas.

Holding true to the typical NVA ambush tactics, two sappers (enemy soldiers, similar to the Japanese Kamikaze) jumped out of nowhere and started running at us, swinging satchel charges (high explosive bombs) over their heads. The two sappers were the first of many I was forced to kill face-to-face that day. As I handed ammo up to the turret, I had to pick up Marines, dead and alive, and throw them anywhere I could, off the road or onto my Duster. If I didn't pick up and move them, I would have had to drive over them as we advanced. That was something I would not allow myself to do, even if it meant dying trying to move them. The Squad Leaders were always getting pissed off at me for not obeying Duster combat orders about not picking up the dead and wounded during a battle. However, I thought I was quick enough to hand out ammo, advance the Duster, do radio communications, kill the Gooks, and still load the wounded on the back of the Duster and move the dead out of the way of my track. On the other hand, running over "Dinks" was good luck.

The battle was very smoky, extremely hectic, and frightening beyond comprehension. The **"INCOMING!"** and shooting seemed endless. The noise was deafening and droning. Over the sounds of war, I could hear the screams of the wounded and dying from both sides. As I pulled out a can of ammo, there was a loud explosion and I was thrown against the Duster. Everything inside me went into slow motion recovery mode. As they say, my bell was rung (for the first time) and I was on a super adrenaline rush trying to regroup and shake off the cobwebs.

I got wounded for the first time. A long piece of toothpick thin shrapnel was sticking through my left side at my waist, in the area I called my "spare tire". The hot sliver was just under the skin but was too painful to remove when I tried to pull it out. My arms had what looked like hundreds of little needles in them, with small smears of blood everywhere. Death and destruction was all around us. I knew I had to keep humping ammo, driving forward, picking up Marines, and staying focused. We were now all operating on adrenaline and trying to stay alive. Killing the NVA was at another all-time high. I had emptied my ammo can full of grenades into the brush on each side of the road. No Gooks were going to take my track or me, or cut off my balls. Muzzle flashes from some kind of NVA artillery could be seen coming from the surrounding hills. I radioed for our own artillery support. Over the radio, we heard Wayne Bailey, from our Second Platoon, advising us that he could see with his binoculars part of the ambush from his hill position at The Rockpile. Bailey also advised us he could see the small flags tied to our whip antennas above the elephant grass. I radioed Bailey and asked him to shoot high and over us into the hills. In less than a minute, Bailey's crew, via our Squad Leaders radio commands, swept the ridgeline with effective 40mm counter-fire, hitting the enemy and getting secondary explosions. In a flash, the firefight was over. We sat poised for another rush. I could see dead NVA lying in the grass, and some wounded and trying to crawl away. *A shot was fired and another NVA soldier stopped crawling forever.*

Marines, trained to perfection, instantly began regrouping. Within minutes the Marine lieutenant in charge had the convoy back on the road to Ca Lu. Vehicles towed vehicles. It was an everyday occurrence to them and they acted professionally. A Marine Corpsman dressed my wounds. He leaned me against the Duster and bent the long piece of shrapnel around my waist. Now at least I could sit in the Driver's seat without pain. The Corpsman hitched a ride on our Duster and told me I was lucky that the shrapnel in me was just under the skin and had stopped bleeding. I wasn't going to die and it was only a flesh wound. He advised me to have a doctor remove it back at Carroll. As I drove, the Corpsman climbed back and forth over the Duster, administering aid to his fellow Marines we carried. The Corpsman's courage and caring was beyond admiration. Medics and Corpsman were the Messiahs of the combat field. I had a saying, "Corpsman and Medic's held two hands, yours and God's." We arrived at Ca Lu about two hours late. As if nothing serious had happened, we exchanged quick firefight stories, said our hellos to the Duster crews at Ca Lu, replenished the ammo, and headed back to Carroll with three trucks.

At Carroll, I was taken to the back south end of the camp to the Medivac Station where a doctor tended to my wounds. It was the area's head Triage Center. They did not ask your name or unit. Like an assembly line, the lesser wounded were bandaged and the severely wounded were airlifted off of the base. I became unraveled when a

Priest approached me and started giving me what I thought were my last rites. "Father, the Corpsman told me I only had a flesh wound and now you think I am dying?" I freaked and told him if he continued I would have to shoot him and wasn't ready to die yet. When the doctor finally approached me, he looked in amazement at the piece of shrapnel wrapped around me. I assured him it was only a flesh wound and was only just under the skin, probably less than 1/8" of an inch. He told some other doctor-type guys or Corpsman to ship me to Dong Ha. That put me over the edge. I told them I was not going to Dong Ha and, after a short but loud argument he agreed they would treat me. Now, totally out of control, I insisted on knowing how they were going to remove MY Shrapnel. The Priest approached me again, trying to console me. "Father, please go the fuck away." I refused to lie down and now stood in the corner. After an hour or so, a guy who looked like a mechanic showed up with a bolt cutter. After a lot of coaxing, I allowed them to cut off the back portion of the shrapnel. The doctor told me he was going to slowly pull out the last piece of metal and for me to stand real still and try to take a deep breath. My stomach turned and I almost passed out. Now on a stretcher, they cleaned out my wounds, used some glue-type substance and butterfly bandages, and sent me on my way. I feel like a real asshole for how I acted.

October 4: We headed out to Dong Ha, one Duster and a truck driven by my friend, Tank. His truck was full of less seriously wounded men who were sitting alongside or on top of their dead friends, just another one of our common medivac runs. It would be a full speed non-stop run down Route 9. We all ran with no governors on our engines. All of the wounded would be checked out, including me, at the main medical station known as Delta Med. The dead would be dropped off at Graves Registration. I think Tank carried more wounded and dead on his truck than any person on the DMZ. He would say, "Joey, this job fuckin' sucks!"

We have a saying, "Who cares?...Only the Rats."

After I got back, I heard that Bailey's crew got a "royal ass chewing" for shooting without permission to fire. As far as we were concerned, they had saved our butts.

Years later, Wayne Bailey and his wife, Dixie, visited my home. The old "Beetle" (his nickname) glowed as he told my family how he saved my life.

October 5: We returned to Carroll with a truckload of new guys. A new Section Chief named Noel Brown, a transferee from another southern Duster unit, was in charge of the Newbees. They were all given the traditional initiation: one hand grenade for the ride and the customary speech about the NVA cutting off their balls. Now, after scaring them shitless, we took them down Route 9.

October 6: We acquired a new guy named Joe Presley. We are ordered to rebuild the roof of our bunker because some big lieutenant named Mitchum hit his head on the doorway and got knocked out trying to run for cover during **"INCOMING!"** We never have any trouble ducking into the doorway. I guess all the footprints on his back, from all of us running over him when he got knocked out, were too much for his ego. Someone has to pay. He got even. The roof job was a real ball buster. As we finished the roof, we watched the B52s bomb the ridgeline of Dong Ha Mountain.

October 7: We made some mine sweeps in the morning. I paid my last installment to Tyrrell Jewelers in California for some gold four leaf clover good luck pins I purchased for my Mom and Dad. I also got a package of goodies from my sister Brenda and her husband Ken, but there's been no mail from my girl, Nancy, in four days. It was my turn to burn the shitter.

The thought still brings a smile to my face. Burn and stir, until shit turns to ash. What a fucking terrible, nasty job! I hate the smell of gasoline and diesel fuel to this day.

Dear Diary,

UNDERLINE

I still remember when I first saw the flash of lightning. Heard and felt the roar of thunder. As a little boy I thought there could be nothing on earth as frightening. Hugging the pillow and taking shelter under the blankets. It was the best protection I could get. I always loved those blankets...
Until I went to Nam...Now they cover my lost friends.

October 8: On our way to do a search and destroy mission with the Marines, we dropped off Section Chief Brown and a few new guys at Delta-5 (D-5), an old French Fort south of Carroll. The fort was surrounded by a mine field and a dry moat filled with punji sticks (sharpened bamboo sticks). It had concrete walls to live in. It was a mud hole when it rained. Plus, it was full of rats. When we got back to our bunker, we cleaned our M-16 and I helped build a half-ass door for the bunker. Still no mail from my Nancy, but I got a goody package from my sister, Brenda. I shared it with my friends. Hopefully, they won't tell me I have KP in the morning.

October 9: The day was business as usual with mine sweeps and trips to the old deserted plantations to cut down little green bananas and pick pineapples. I liked to go there. Before we cut the bananas, we have to hit the banana tree leaves with the flat side of the machete to get rid of the hand-sized spiders and green bamboo viper snakes. We were preparing for another visit to D-5, complete with rations, ammo and water. There, I shared some bananas with my old friends, Lou Block, Norman Oss, Don Wolfe, Steve Harris and their crews. The guys loved my bananas and pineapples. We all laughed when they told us how Section Chief Brown found Norman's Spider Monkey, Lester, in their Duster's turret playing with the hand grenades. Norman told Brown it was Wolfe's monkey and he would gladly get rid of the nasty little bastard. Wolfe got an ass-chewing and Norman hid his monkey on the other side of the camp with a Marine friend. Lester is their mascot.

Many years later, at a reunion, we told Noel Brown that it was Norman's monkey and he had Lester until he went home in August. We all had a good laugh. "Lester...You Stinky Little Bastard, thanks for breaking the monotony of war."

After we returned from D-5, they had us take position up on Observation Post Hill 250. We had our nightly H&I fire mission called to us on the lima-lima (land line or telephone) from the Fire Direction Control Center at Camp Carroll. We wrote down the coordinates, elevations, rounds to be fired, and hourly times of firing. Our Duster fired three-hundred rounds at various pre-planned locations.

October 10: At 0200 hours we got a radio call from Steve Harris' track, C132, stationed at D-5. The ARVNs (Army of the Republic of Vietnam), who shared the fort, had fragged (thrown hand grenades at) some of the Marines stationed there. Harris said the Duster crews had placed all the ARVNs in the center of the fort and wanted to open fire, but were awaiting a reply and orders. At daylight our track and another, along with some Marines and ARVN advisers, arrived at D-5. The matter seemed to be quickly resolved and the fraggers were taken away. The compound at D-5 had lots of problems. Sharing the fort with the ARVNs was not what you would call easy duty. There never seemed to be enough trust about on whose side of the war the ARVNs were fighting.

We were informed, when we got back to Hill 250, that we had killed two and seriously wounded eight villagers from Cam Lo. Our butts were on the line and we had to prove to the officer quizzing us that the Fire Direction Control gave us the fire mission. It was easy to prove it wasn't our fault. Duster standard procedure was writing down all night fire missions. ***Sorry, Captain, go hang one of your FDC jerkoffs!***

October 11: Duster C132 broke down on maneuvers. They had to retrieve it and tow it back to Carroll for repairs. Back at camp, my Nancy's letters finally caught up to me.
I am very happy. I sniffed her perfumed letters on and off for hours

before opening them. I love reading them over and over again. They bring me closer to her and home.

October 12: We continued doing what Dusters do best: running convoys and mine sweeps from Dong Ha to Khe Sanh while being mortared, rocketed, and shot at as we killed the NVA along the way.

October 13: The Duster crews are always changing personnel and reorganizing to give the new men experience. Replacements are needed because men are rotating back to the States or because of death, injury or just plain incompetence. I inquired about my missing personnel records and was advised that they had been reconstructed, but payroll still had to be updated. I elected to receive a Quarter Master Allowance of $50 pay per month. They will send the balance home to my family to bank for me, since I have no place to spend money, but they had no idea when I would get paid.

I always wondered how they could reconstruct my files without asking me any questions.

We saw ***Puff the Dragon*** (C147 plane equipped with Gatling guns) shoot NVA all night. What a display of firepower!

While at Camp Carroll, we stopped at the Mess Hall for some hot chow. I can never get all the flour bugs out of the homemade bread. I make them disappear with jelly. That same asshole food-stirring Marine sat across from us and started his usual routine with our food and his wise-ass remarks. Stirring his finger in each of my guys' meals and laughing, my crew just looked at me for some kind of assistance. They didn't want to start anything with their Marine friends. Very politely, I asked him if he would please stop fucking with my crew. "We hardly get a hot meal and just want to eat, leave, and have no trouble. It's not a joke and you're not funny and if you don't stop I'm going to teach you some fuckin' manners." "And what kind of manners are you going to teach me, Pussy?" Like lightning striking, I stabbed his right hand to the plywood table with my good old Army issue heavy-duty fork. Before he could even react, I quickly reached over the table and grabbed the S.O.B. by the back of his head, slammed his head down on the table, and pulled him real close to my chest. Then I grasped his throat with my right hand and squeezed his larynx real tight with my four fingers and thumb, so he couldn't scream or breathe. I thought for some silly reason nobody would notice me taking out this jerk. I knew I had his sorry ass and it would only take a minute for his lights to be out. He slumped and started to twitch. My crew quickly pulled me off him before he stopped breathing forever. Nobody bitched, complained, or said anything as his Marine friends dragged him out of our Mess Hall. We finished eating, smiling at each other between bites. The other guys in the Mess Hall just stared at us as we slowly walked out drinking chocolate milk. I didn't even get in trouble. It's the Nam.

October 14: We took an empty 50 gallon drum that had contained the defoliant (Agent Orange) we used to keep the weeds down around our position. With an ax and a hammer, we cut the barrel in half long ways. We now have our own little bath tub and a place to wash our clothes. It is great. Lighting a small fire underneath gave us hot water. One of the guys used a small pail and, as we squatted, he poured the hot water over our head. A quick lather of soap, some splashing, another pail of water, and bath time was over. In less than thirty minutes, the five of us had a bath. We took turns being "guy number 5". Then, that same bath water was used to wash our clothes.

October 15: We escorted a truck loaded with medical supplies out to the Ayd Station at Ca Lu. Lt. Moore told us that the medical station was named after the Marine Jacques J. Ayd, who was a Corpsman with Ripley's Raiders and was killed by NVA artillery at Ca Lu. He was right behind Don Wolfe's Duster position when the shell hit. Captain John Ripley had the Montagnards build a thatched building as the medical evacuation center for this area. Besides treating Americans, the Yards could get medical assistance. On June 22, 1967, he had our Dusters escort the Marine Corps Band out to the building for a formal dedication ceremony. He said it was amazing to see the Yards hear a band play for the first time in their lives. He always thought that a few in attendance were NVA soldiers. Who else but the Marines would send their band into the combat zone? Those poor guys had to be scared shitless.

October 19: I told the guys it is my girlfriend Nancy's 20th birthday. We sang "Happy Birthday" to her. I re-read her letters. I have sniffed all the perfume off of them.

I hope to get a new scent soon. It is funny how we pass around each other's unopened letters trying to guess the name of the perfume. We came up with all kinds of silly sexual names. If you sniffed another guy's letter too long, they'd get pissed off.

October 20: I dreaded body recovery. Being one of the newer guys, I have to pick up all the pieces. The dead have to meet God with all their parts. It is the task from Hell. If the men are severely wounded, I give them morphine to ease their pain. If they are dying and time allows, I hold them and comfort them until the chariot from Heaven arrives. I owe this to their mothers and my own salvation.

October 21: The medic at Camp Carroll had me airlifted to the hospital in Da Nang to get my jungle rot treated. The Mycelex cream ointment he had given me previously was not working and my legs had about twenty oozing holes in them about 3/8" round and a 1/2" deep. My crotch had a purple rash, and the skin was peeling.

October 22: The hospital is great; hot showers, great food, a bed and clean clothes. While the doctors and nurses cleaned my rot, I had to help the wounded soldiers and Marines. I was considered one of the "Walking Wounded". Our tasks included everything from mopping floors to changing bed pans and pushing gurneys.

I cannot believe that they had wounded NVA in the same room as our wounded. The wounded NVA had a military policeman guarding them. The cop never said a thing or even gave a glance as the Marine in the bed next to the Gook pulled out his intravenous lines. I just kept mopping.

October 23: The funniest thing happened today. In the morning they had the entire Walking Wounded stand in formation in front of a nurse. There we were, all in our hospital gowns with our asses hanging out. There were about thirty of us standing tall, ten across and three rows deep. The nurse started telling us about a parasite that was in the river water that could have gotten up into our colon through our anus. She then pointed to a cart full of small soup size paper cups with lids. She announced that she wanted each one of us to label a container with our name and service number, defecate into the container and return it to the cart. We all stood there staring at the cart, thinking "This is nuts." One of the brothers chirped up and said, "Excuse me Mams. Did I hear you right? You want us to pinch one off into that little cup?" Everyone burst into laughter. The poor embarrassed nurse started yelling and handing out cups, screaming if we didn't do what she said we could not go back to our units. That sounded great to us, we all threw the cups in the garbage and walked away laughing. Twenty minutes later we were all back in formation. Standing in front of us was a Colonel wearing bloody surgical scrubs. At the top of his lungs he spoke a language we all understood. "Listen you assholes! You will take one of those fucking cups, write your name and service number on it, and take a shit in it! I don't care if you shit in your hands, or pants, or dig it out of your asshole with a tongue depressor, but that cup will be filled and placed back on that fucking cart! Do you maggots understand me?!" All you heard was a big "Hoo Rah, Colonel," as we all snapped to attention and saluted. The nurse just stood there smiling.

October 25: Before going back to the DMZ, the hospital took us over to a large PX and USO Center. It was a relaxing day of playing games and picking up some needed toiletries. They had a place that sold Zippo lighters and you could get them engraved for a dollar. I bought a new Zippo and had it engraved "To Really Live – You Must Nearly Die". It was crazy, because the guy standing in front of me in line was a hometown friend named Tony Zelec who was in the Marines. As we waited to get our lighters engraved, I told him I had seen John Driscoll, another Marine from our town, playing baseball up in Dong Ha. Talking to Tony was a nice change of pace.

October 26: To forget we are in a war, we are always having some kind of card game, knife throwing contest, shooting contest, or boxing and wrestling. Today, we started a new type of knife throwing contest. Instead of throwing at a small wooden target leaning against or nailed to a pole, we took turns holding the target. What a rush! You just stood there while a guy threw his knife at you and you followed the knife to the wood. If the knife went off target, you quickly moved the target to the knife. If it hit you, so what, maybe you'd go home.

October 27: The crew helped me tension the track treads. We need the Duster to run straight and true. Sometimes we don't come to a complete stop while shooting. I need the Duster to go perfectly straight as I let her chug down the road at a slow jerky pace, so I can hand out ammo from the Driver's hatch.

October 28: After a few days of having lots of fun and laughs, Lt. Moore caught us at our new knife throwing contest. Screaming and yelling, he called us a bunch of sickos and said this was not what he expected of his men. One of the guys laughed and told him it was the Army's new type of agility drill. Moore did not like his humor and told us if he found us doing something crazy like that again, he would ship us off to another unit. We all looked at each other and smiled…No knives?...How 'bout axes?

October 31: Halloween…I cannot help but think of how I survived another month killing all kinds of goblins and scary creatures of the night. Would I make it through this night or would the Devil come calling for my soul? No…The Devil was already here.

Ca Lu

*"The Razorback Mountain" part of the mountains made up of
"The Rockpile" and "Fish Bowl" area. On top of the Razorback is a
Marine lookout position, only accessible by helicopter.*

Heading out to the Fish Bowl.

Our bunker on Hill 250. This is where Lt. Mitchum hit his head.

The new bunker Lt. Mitchum made my crew build.

Delta – 5

Delta – 5 Punji Pit

Duster at Delta – 5

Bananas

Norman Oss and Joe Belardo.
Norman was the best driver in the 1/44 Artillery.

"Lester" the monkey

Bath time

The Marine Corps band playing at the dedication of the Ayd Station.

Ayd station dedication – the Montagnard people had never seen or heard a band. The tall guys were suspected NVA-Chinese advisors enjoying the music.

I carried this picture of my fiancée, Nancy, throughout Vietnam.

The spectacular view and firing advantage from Hill 250.

*Secondary explosions were seen from Hill 250 after hitting enemy
positions on the eastern slope of Dong Ha mountain.*

Hill 250 ground-artillery radar surveillance.

*A pile of 40mm empty brass ammo casings, lying on the ground
After only one minute of shooting at an NVA position.*

CHAPTER 5: AND HELL CAME CALLING

<u>**November 1:**</u> Sgt. Dieter took Russia Holley and me with him to Ca Lu. After a few days, Dieter will leave to return home to the United States and we will return to The Rockpile.

<u>**November 2:**</u> Today, our Squad Leader, Eugene Triola, got bitten by a rat. I feel sorry for him because he only has a few days left before he is to return home and he has to get two weeks of rabies shots before he can leave.

His instant replacement is a dumb-ass guy we immediately nickname Dufuss. We are not happy with this sergeant as our Squad Leader. In addition, the LT sent orders to swap two experienced men for two other experienced men. Our crew now consists of me as the Driver, Gunner Joe Musso, Gun Bunnies Cleave Lanier and Russia Holly, and Dufuss.

We started running north of The Rockpile, past our North OP (Observation Post) to a place they called "The Fish Bowl". Our job was to escort Marines to and from this tiny outpost situated between three high peaks, north of the highest mountain peak called The Razor Back, west of what they called Mutters Ridge. It was a shooting gallery for the NVA and a nightmare of a place for anyone. A Marine or two would always get wounded or killed on each trip. When we returned to The Rockpile, we put the KIAs next to the Landing Zone pad situated on the east edge of the camp on a lower flat area just below our Duster position. It was the official ***"Tag and Bag"*** area. I heard the Marine Priest singing "Simeon's Chant" again to the dead. I hated him and his song. It makes the war become a reality; it makes me vulnerable, it makes me think. And that type of thinking will get me killed.

Twenty years passed and, at my Uncle Henry's funeral, a young Irish Priest sang. His words of Simeon were more than a flashback. My mind and soul melted, I cried, sobbed, and shook out of control as the priest chanted. My relatives thought it was for Uncle Henry.

November 3: We all examined the hole in Cleve Lanier's helmet. Cleve told us this horrifying story of how he got shot in the head and how his helmet saved him. "The bullet hit my helmet, went through, and cut my head right here. It continued to travel between the plastic helmet liner and metal outside and exited right here," he explained.

It was a miracle he survived.

Don Wolfe continued the story and told us the battle had taken place on August 30th. A convoy heading back from Ca Lu to the Rockpile was hit by the NVA. Don's Duster, commanded by Squad Leader Sgt. Laurier Derosier, went out to help them. Trying to rescue the Marines, they fought their way into the fire fight. Because of the carnage on the road, they were forced to stop. Their Duster was now stopped on an elevated section of Route 9 surrounded by elephant grass. Because of their position, it was impossible to lower the 40s enough to shoot real close and clear the area of NVA. Cleve said Don grabbed the M60 and started blasting away at the advancing NVA. The NVA then turned their focus on the Duster. RPGs started flying overhead, and enemy automatic weapon bullets began feverishly pinging off the Duster. One of the bullets hit Cleve in the helmet and sent him flying and another hit Derosier in the head, severely wounding him. Because of the ferocity of the battle, they were unable to give aid to Laurier until after the battle. Still alive, he was dropped off at The Rockpile by the crew along with the other wounded and dead. They hope their friend will survive from his horrible head wound.

November 4: The Battalion Commander, Lieutenant Colonel John House, came to Camp Carroll and fired Charlie Battery's 200,000th 40mm cannon shell. The Chaplain, Captain Cecil Lewis, assisted. It confirmed our suspicions that our battery was in deep heavy contact with the NVA. Almost a quarter of a million 40mm cannon shells had been fired at the NVA. *How many did I help kill?*

November 5: Sgt. Dufuss, our new Squad Leader, always becomes unraveled during **"INCOMING!"** and loses his leadership ability during firefights. We have get to get rid of this guy.

November 6: Lt. Moore was reassigned to Charlie Battery Headquarters. Our Section has been taken over by a new lieutenant named Lt. Hardin. Our Duster crew is not sure of the new lieutenant. He has never been tested under enemy fire. Whatever stateside jungle training tactics he had is a far cry from the Vietnam Conflict and doesn't work. We will try to teach him the ropes and hopefully keep him alive. We also agree that we will override his orders during combat if they jeopardize the mission.

November 7: Two NVA cannon shells landed next to our bunker. What an explosion!
I thought we had taken a direct hit. Debris was everywhere. A few of us were thrown up into the air and flung against the walls by the concussion of the blast. Our ears rang and are bleeding. It shook the hell out of us. Our bodies hurt and we have black and blues all over.

November 8: We escorted a truck full of C-Rations, water, and ammo out to a little outpost north of The Rockpile called the North OP. We have one Duster crew there and a platoon of Marines. My friends Norman Oss, Daryl Hale and Billy Conley were part of the Duster crew. It was good to see my old friends. As I approached Norman, his monkey Lester jumped on my shoulder and as quick as lightning opened my shirt pocket and pulled out my last Tareyton cigarette and ate it. I tried to grab him and he bit me. Then, he reached in my pocket again and took out my last piece of Juicy Fruit chewing gum and ate that. I quickly pulled him by his leash, tossed him to the ground, stepped on him, pulled out my .45 pistol, and was going to blow his brains out. Norman started screaming, "Jooooe! Noooooo! Please don't kill my son! He is the heir to my throne!"
I couldn't help but laugh. I let him go and the little bastard took a quick shit and threw it at me. Everybody became hysterical with laughter. Lester was a hard act to follow.

Years after the war, Norman would settle in Coeur d'Alene, Idaho. To promote peace and harmony, Norman hand carves beautiful walking sticks for all ages. He hands out, free of cost, over 1500 sticks per year. The town blog calls him "The Stickman".

November 10: We installed a new engine in C141. The job took about three hours. We then went down to the river and washed the dried blood and parts from the wounded and dead off the Duster. I couldn't help but cry. I am constantly picking up wounded and dead. They call us "The Body Snatchers". The feeling of their blood becoming sticky and drying on my skin makes me unbelievably sad. I can't help but stare at myself as it dries and turns burnt reddish brown on my hands and clothes. My friend's life blood dries under my fingernails. I can't stand how they look and clean them constantly with my knife. ***God, please save me.***

November 11: A Duster crew from the other side of our combat base observed lights from NVA moving along the perimeter. The lights were extinguished with a minute long burst of our 40mm guns.

November 12: Our track C141 was not running well, so the LT ordered us to swap Dusters with Lou Block. We had to keep running the road to Ca Lu or some other God-forsaken place. Lou was not happy.

November 13: Still raining, still eating C-Rations, and we are all still scared shitless. We had to drive through three or four feet of mud to get into Ca Lu. What a mud hole! The mud was so deep, it pulled our boots off as we walked. We took turns with the bulldozer, pushing the trucks and other vehicles through the deep thick mud.

I heard my own confession and gave myself absolution, reciting three Hail Mary's. God won't mind. Some days I feel like the Devil is taking over my body and soul.

November 14: We ran Route 9 past Ca Lu to a place called Joliet. Route 9 was always scary because the elephant grass grew high and thick, right up to the edge of the road. Charlie could just step out of the grass and let you have it. The road smelled from all the dead NVA we killed on our trips up and down it. They keep coming and we keep killing.

November 16: Lt. Hardin had a meeting with our crew. He called our crew "rebels and trouble makers" and is tired of us not listening to him and overriding his orders. We explained to him that we are only trying to stay alive and keep him alive. He does not have enough combat experience yet and should learn to listen to the more experienced crews. We told him not to be drawn into the ambush, stay outside if possible, counter fire, and see if he could get any enemy return fire. Eliminate them and pick other targets. "Remember, Sir, we can't shoot closer than 88 feet. If the Duster is caught in the center of an ambush without first counter firing, it will be destroyed. Under 88 feet you have to use the machine gun, grenades and rifles, and reposition the Duster on the sloped banks of the road to be able to shoot lower and closer." Somehow our discussion, which we thought was going on the positive note, turned into an argument and screaming match. He told us that he was the officer in charge and we had to listen to him. Again he called us "rebels" and told us he was going to give us all the road duty. That's okay with us, because we already do all the road duty. We could not figure what went wrong with our meeting. We were just trying to help the new lieutenant.

November 17: We got C141 back from Lou. The engine now ran great, but the starter was broken. They told us to jump-start it and drive it anyway. What a joke!

November 18: Ambush Alley kept its reputation. The truck in front of us was hit square with an RPG from the left side of the road. Trying to block the road was a typical NVA tactic. The Marines scrambled for the nearest cover, the right side of our now stationary Duster. I could feel the Duster as it rocked from what felt like two explosions. The Duster had not yet begun firing. I thought we were hit, but the Duster was still running. I emptied my M-16 into a few Gooks running at us with satchel charges. The charges exploded and Gook parts flew everywhere. Again, there was another explosion. Dirt, debris and smoke now covered our Duster. Joe Musso started screaming into the headset, "The Sarge is freaking out, won't shoot, and is rolling grenades off the right side of our Duster, blowing up Marines!" I frantically climbed out of the Driver's hatch and up to the turret. I grabbed Sgt. Dufuss, threw him onto the rear deck of the Duster, and gave him a quick slap to the face that knocked him on his ass. I told Cannoneer Lanier to get the fucking guns shooting. I gave the injured Marines the best aid I could and placed them on the rear deck of the Duster. I told the Sarge to hold on to them and not to fuck up or I'd kill him.

We dropped the Marines off at the Ayd Station. Later today, we heard that two Marines had died in the battle and many others had been wounded. I prayed that our sergeant was not responsible for any of their deaths.

November 20: This evening, Sgt. Dufuss ran his mouth about his triumphs of the other day's battle. I went crazy and wanted what I called "a piece of the Old Sarge". Before I could grab him and kick his ass, he retreated to the confines of our bunker. I started screaming for him to come out of the bunker, so I could kick his butt "Jersey style" all over the camp. The rest of the crew started getting just as crazy. The sergeant wouldn't come out, but continued to heckle us about the battle. We all charged into the bunker. Pushing the Sarge up against the dirt wall, I pressed my M-16 against his forehead and announced that chicken shits, cowards, and assholes had no place on our track and that it was his turn to die. Lanier grabbed the gun and stopped me from killing the bastard.

I quickly hit the Sarge with a few hard punches. He slumped to the dirt floor, lights out. I became hysterical and retreated to the confines of my Driver's compartment, my private sanctuary. We were a team and the team was having troubles. I did not want to die because someone screwed up and I wasn't going to put up with his shit. Back in the bunker I announced, "If the Sarge fucks up again, just shoot him. Only listen to Musso and me." I then proceeded to beat his ass again. Nobody said anything. They knew better.

November 21: Lt. Hardin got us another Duster C131, "The Track from Hell." He told us C141 needed its engine rebuilt again. We needed a good running Duster to keep us running Route 9. The LT asked the Sarge how he got all busted up. The Sarge was smart and told him he fell off the Duster during night Guard Duty and hit his face and head. I just shrugged and smiled.

November 24: We heard that Con Thien was half overrun by the NVA. We continued the run to Ca Lu, the crew praying that the Sarge wouldn't screw up again. I began to hate two things: the NVA, and the Sarge.

Wayne Bailey came back from the hospital after a bout with malaria. Sergeant Noel Brown got bitten three times by a rat. A tiger bit a Marine on the arm. He became a celebrity. Lou Block became the driver of C121. The original men I came to Carroll with are just starting to get a taste of the road.

I finally received my Quarter Master Allowance. I got paid $182.00 and sent $160.00 home to Mom. To get money, I have been selling surgical alcohol mixed with Lemon-Lime Kool-Aid. I call it a Jungle Daiquiri. Unbelievably, some asshole from Headquarters called me on the radio and asked if I knew where my personnel records were, because they are missing. **How would I know, you dumb shit?**

November 26: The Sarge was finally replaced and no one ever said another thing about "Dufuss." Joe Musso has become our Squad Leader. Chester Sines was promoted to Staff Sergeant E-6 and has become our new section chief. I know Chester will make the best Section Chief in the 44th. This is the beginning of the makings of another great fighting team.

The NVA tried to hit the top of the outpost known as "The Razorback". We continue to run the road.

November 28: Battalion announced that we have held our positions on the DMZ for one full year. By now, all of the original party that had come to Vietnam with the 1/44th had completed their tours of duty and were going home. The only year I wanted to celebrate was completing the twelve months I had to serve, allowing me to go home too.

"The Rockpile"
Duster position can be seen in upper right.
Two Quad-50's can be seen driving though camp.

Another new engine for the Duster.

Marine resupply truck heading down muddy Route 9 to Ca Lu.

Bulldozer pushing Duster fuel truck through mud at Ca Lu.

The Rockpile LZ and Graves Registration area.
Marines can be seen waiting to load a helicopter.
The Marines' chaplain would stand next to the Marine guard position
in foreground and chant his prayers and song.

Medivac

CHAPTER 6: A DEADLY DECEMBER

December 2: The Dusters and Quad-50s engaged a large NVA unit at Camp Carroll. The Dusters shot over 950 rounds of 40mm cannon shells and the Quad-50s shot 2,200 rounds of 50-caliber machine gun ammo. It was just another busy day at the office for my people. We blew the shit out of the NVA. Parts and bodies were all over the place. It felt good to get even with those little bastards. They were left to rot where they fell.

December 3: We heard that Sergeant Derosier died from the head wounds he had received in the August 30th battle. I prayed that God would rest his soul. He will be sadly missed, especially by Don Wolfe, Cleve Lanier, Cooper Thomas and Leslie "Red" Dietze.

December 5: I was called to an awards' formation regarding the October 3rd battle. After the formation had assembled, I was asked to step out of the awards line. I was told there must have been an error. It was very humiliating. The officer in charge of the awards ceremony made it seem like I was stealing someone's day of fame and glory. I told him where he could stick it. He just smiled. I then told him to get fucked and smiled back.

December 6: We went back to Carroll to pick up our new medic. Via the radio, we were told he was one brave son-of-a-bitch and fearless. His name was James "Doc" Butler. After a brief introduction, Doc gave me another crash lesson on medical aid and treatment on the combat field. After my two hour session, the LT asked me to take Doc to The Rockpile, so he could meet the other combat teams and give them a little extra medical training.

Since Doc had never been in any combat on the road, I went over some basic survival skills with him before heading back to The Rockpile. I wanted Doc to sit next to me on the TC's seat of our Duster. However, I explained to him that I had taken out the seat and replaced it with 40mm ammo cans surrounded by lots of loose ammo. The entire Driver's compartment now carried ammo and the only place to really sit was my Driver's seat. It was tough sitting for the rider, but I wanted all the ammo I could carry. On top of the can I had placed two flak jackets for the rider to sit on.

I told Doc, that if anything should happen, he should stay real low, with only his eyes sticking out above the rim of his side of the compartment, and to shoot only at confirmed targets. To my surprise, he announced that he was only there to save people and not to kill them and was more than willing to die trying to save lives. Looking into his eyes, I knew he was not lying and had convictions of steel. I quickly inspected the M14 rifle he carried. I wanted to make sure that if I needed to use it, it was loaded and ready to shoot. There was no ammo in it and the barrel was full of dirt. "I just carry it because I was ordered to." Nodding and shrugging my shoulders, I told him to get in the Duster. I did not know what to do, so I handed him one of my hand grenades and instructed him to throw it on my order. In a firm, no nonsense voice I said "Doc, when I say "throw", you throw as far as you can and then get low and out of sight. I don't care if you don't want to kill another human, you're on my Duster and we don't fuck around. If you want all of us to live, you best throw that fuckin' grenade when I tell you. Be careful, the pins are partially straightened, so it will be real easy to pull and throw. Hopefully nothing will happen."

As we road down Route 9 to The Rockpile, we received a few enemy sniper rounds and small arms fire, but just kept riding and only shot back with our M60 machine gun. Doc, ducking from the bullets pinging off the Duster, accidentally dropped his hand grenade into my pile of loose 40mm ammo. He shouted to me that he could see the grenade rolling all over the Duster floor under all the ammo. I started laughing and yelling, "What a fucking way to die! Doc, get down there and find that fucking grenade and make sure the pin does not pull out." I was the lead Duster in the "Rough Rider Convoy" and was traveling at 45 miles per hour down Route 9's winding, bumpy road. Dusters only stop when the convoy gets really hit by the enemy and needs our fire power. Otherwise, we just keep going to our destination, driving through the shooting gallery like sitting ducks. Doc, screaming and fishing through the ammo, finally found the grenade. Showing it to me in triumph, I quickly grabbed it, bent the pull pin tight and handed it back as if nothing happened, yelling "Keep your head down!"

At The Rockpile, I introduced Doc to the other guys and instructed him that he would be living with them in the small bunker next to our Command Post. In the morning, I will take him to meet the rest of the guys at The Rockpile.

December 7: I told the crew I will be getting married to my girl, Nancy, one year from this day. David Lewis arrived in the morning and became our new Cannoneer. I took Doc around and introduced him to the other guys from the 44th and his counterparts, the Marine Corpsmen. We still run Ambush Alley every day. Death and destruction, living and dying, melts into one everyday occurrence. My God, I have only been in Nam a little more than three months. Will my Nancy think I have changed? Will my family hate me for what I have done?

December 8: Six days a week, I have guard duty and hate every minute. It is lonely and very frightening. Each day before Guard Duty I set up my position, changing the place I sit every night. In the daylight hours, I check out what is in front of my position and make small stone replicas of the trees, brush, and hills. In the dark I can feel the rocks and stare into the midnight shadows hoping nothing has moved. It's amazing how the NVA disguise themselves as trees and brush and move up on me. With just a feel, I can always account for what is in front of me. I keep the safety off my M-16. I don't want the enemy to hear it click on, if I need to shoot. Any added objects to my field of view automatically get shot. I never sit in or on the Duster. It is a prime target. Each night I sneak up to the Duster and place a helmet on the sighting rings. From a distance it looks like you are sitting in the Duster. You just sit, wait, and pray nothing happens. I can out sit a mouse. It's amazing what you hear or think you hear, and when the shadows move…**OOOh, shit!!**

December 10: Joe Musso and I shared a small bottle of Mogen David Wine that my Aunt Margie sent me for Christmas. We sat in our bunker by a Christmas tree his mother sent, sipping the wine and eating the popcorn the wine had been packed in to protect it from breakage on its long flight from home. They tasted great together.

December 11: Joe Musso left Nam for his home in Union, New Jersey. When he gets home, he promised to visit my family and tell them that everything is okay, not to worry, and that I am in a fairly safe area. Only a Nam brother can look into another soldier's mother's face and lie that good.

Today Joe is a firefighter in his hometown. He can't stop saving others.

December 12: Sam Lewis, a very quiet man from Oklahoma, with some combat experience, became our Squad Leader.

December 14: Earl "Tex" Holt became our other new Cannoneer. He was my personal pick out of all the guys. Tex is big, about 6'-2". I told him he will be my main cannon loader and I expect him to load both guns while the other loader shoots the machine gun. I warned him not to disappoint me.

Tex rose to every occasion and never let me down or disappointed me throughout our time together in Nam. He was a Warrior King and is a true friend to this day.

I have begun to worry. We have two new guys and we haven't stopped running Ambush Alley. It turns out that Chester Sines and David Lewis are next door neighbors back in the real world. Chester and I started giving crash combat courses to the two Newbees. We wanted them to quickly understand the life-threatening conditions they are in and that training is of the utmost importance. ***My instinct tells me that they will rise to "Kill the Dragon" and "Duel with the Devil".***

Sam Lewis and I asked Lt. Hardin if our crew could rest a few days before hitting the road again. I don't know exactly what happened but, as usual, our meeting didn't go as planned and I ended up cursing out Lt. Hardin. Sam started yelling at him in some Native American language and I started laughing. I have this loud, wild laugh and get this silly smile and grin. It drives the Lieutenant crazy. We just walked away, cursing him out in Native American and my broken Italian.

December 15: We were ordered to rebuild our dilapidated bunker and live in some little, shitty tent.

December 16: Our assignment was another run to Ca Lu and back. The crew of Sam Lewis, Russia Holley, Earl Holt, David Lewis and I are magically able to work as a team. I am amazed how comfortable we are with each other. The crew removed the front plate with our Grim Reaper insignia painted on it from between the 40mm barrels and replaced it with a plain plate. They thought the logo was bad medicine. The only bad omen they could have would be if they ever hesitated to kill. God didn't plan it that way, but someone has to be the Grim Reaper in war. Uncle Sam and the war have trained us too well. Our surroundings make us rise to the occasion. It is kill or be killed, something we have become real good at…too good.

December 19: Another convoy got hit in Ambush Alley. Three trucks and one M48 tank got hit, two Marines were KIA and four were WIA. John Stokes from Charlie Battery, carrying the mail to Ca Lu, was hit real badly through the upper arm. He came back to The Rockpile screaming and looking for help. A portion of his bone was missing. I thought his arm was going to fall off as it swung like a pendulum from side to side. I dressed his wound the best I could and wrapped his arm in a makeshift sling tight to his body. John just stood there bitching and yelling like a wild hillbilly. Stokes was medivaced and never returned. He got his ticket home. Christmas came early for John Stokes.

We headed back to the ambush site under Lt. Moore's leadership and swept the enemy from the area with a volley of 40mm rounds. The enemy small arms and automatic weapons being fired at us were instantly quelled. We then blew up the two destroyed Marine ammo trucks left at the ambush. I don't know for sure what kind of ammo it was, or if the NVA had planted booby traps in the trucks, but it was one hell of an explosion when the trucks blew up. We quickly tucked our heads down into our flak jackets like turtles, as we got pelted by all kinds of debris (dirt, rocks and metal parts of the trucks) bouncing off us and our Duster.

December 20: We returned again with Lt. Moore and helped drag and push the blown up trucks off the road, bringing back any pieces we could find. This afternoon we took out another convoy to Ca Lu, as though nothing had ever happened.

This was Lt. Moore's last ride down Ambush Alley to Ca Lu. He decided we would leave The Rockpile forty minutes before the rest of the convoy. He ordered us to travel at a slow speed and hammer the north and south of the ridgeline with our 40s, hoping to kill the always waiting NVA before they had a chance to get off a shot. About a half mile out, we both noticed a lone tree about ten feet off the road. The crew, engrossed in their shooting mission, never noticed the tree. Before we could stop or yell into our communication helmets, the turret swung and let the tree have it with both barrels. I quickly stopped the Duster. The pieces of the exploding tree bounced back and hit me and Moore. We looked like two giant porcupines with thousands of tiny toothpicks sticking out of us. We climbed out and up to the turret to show the guys what they had done. They became hysterical with laughter, as Moore and I picked out the toothpicks.

I was hoping Moore would stay with us, but he has been reassigned to Charlie Battery's Headquarters section back at Camp Carroll. We are all happy for him that he is leaving "THE ROAD". He had led us well and taught us much. I hope we will meet again someday, stateside, so I can thank him in person for everything he had done for the men and me.

December 21: Lt. Hardin asked for one volunteer from our track for another one of his suicide recovery missions. We cut playing cards to see who would go. The new guy, Tex, pulled an ace. I looked Tex square in the eye, smiled, and announced, "Sorry Earl, you lose, aces are ones in Nam." I looked around the bunker and we were all nodding in total agreement. We all thought that Earl would not be coming back.

Later, on our radio, we had heard one of the guys got killed. We all thought that Tex had bit the bullet. We went through his belongings and divided up his clothes and personal cleaning items. Hours later, to our surprise, Earl returned, only to catch me writing a letter of condolence to his mother and the guys packing his personals to send back to his family. He was even more upset when one of the guys asked him if he wanted his stuff back. The other guys started laughing. I could not help but raise my eyebrows and smile. Tex is very, very religious and insisted we all pray with him and repent our heathen ways. We said a prayer with Tex and listened as he read scriptures to us---his pulpit, a sandbag illuminated by a candle. ***Reality Check.***

December 22: We shot our way back and forth from Ca Lu. No troops were hit, ***Thank God.***

We dropped off some supplies to the Yards living a little past Ca Lu. My heart was broken when I found out that the NVA practiced genocide on the poor Montagnard people. Because Montagnards took aid from the Americans and did not obey the NVA, they killed a few of their children, beheading them and placed their heads on bamboo pikes. The sight was beyond anything I had ever seen. I cried at the very thought that my gifts of Bazooka Bubblegum and candy got those beautiful children killed! Is there a God?! I hate the NVA. I promised the village chief, through hand gestures and body language, that we will revenge their children's deaths. Another broken-hearted memory is born.

December 23: We escorted another convoy to Ca Lu and back to the Rockpile. At Ca Lu we got hit with seventy NVA rockets. We were lucky none hit the convoy staging area. We loaded the trucks with the dead first and then the wounded. Live friends were sitting on top of dead friends. My heart never stops breaking.

To this day, I can never understand why we just didn't take and hold all the roads, hills, and mountains from Dong Ha to Khe Sanh. Why weren't we allowed to fight like they did in other wars? Thousands of soldiers and Marines would have been saved, both physically and mentally. We all knew the military was not running this war, but that some asshole politician, with some liberal asshole reporter stuck up his ass, was in control.

We think that either someone has it in for us, or that we are the best crew around, because we still have not stopped running Ambush Alley.

December 24: Lt. Hardin surprised us and gave us off Christmas Eve and Christmas Day. We had no bunker and are living in a small tent with a candle for light. Joe Musso has left us his mother's small Christmas tree with a box of miniature Christmas balls. We spent the morning decorating our tree. Since we have no tinsel, we unwrapped my eight packs of Juicy Fruit Chewing Gum and twisted the middle so they looked like little bows and added them to our tree. As we dressed our tree, we all sang Christmas Carols. It was contagious. Before we knew it, we had half The Rockpile singing "Jingle Bells." We played cards for matchsticks and lost at horseshoes to a surprisingly agile old sergeant named Cecil Hamilton. The evening was spent sharing some pepperoni and provolone cheese from one of my "CARE" packages and helping Earl tape-record messages to his mother. We took turns giving his mom pre-planned messages about how great Earl was doing and how wonderful it was where we lived. The rest of the night was spent listening to the taped messages she sent Earl and our crew. Her soothing Texas voice made it a wonderful taste of home and a great Christmas Eve gift for all of us.

December 25: It is Christmas Day. Duster crews took turns running to Camp Carroll for a great hot Christmas meal. We rushed down to the river and took a quick bath. We didn't have time to wash our clothes and were forced to celebrate the holiday in our dirty, blood-stained clothes. The cooks did a fantastic job in the mess hall. I could not believe the great assortment of food and all the holiday decorations. As the Soldiers and Marines in the mess hall bowed their heads, Earl said grace. We ended our meal trying to sing a few Christmas songs. Our designated thirty minutes of great chow and good tidings was over. It was time to saddle up and head back to The Rockpile and give the next crew their turn. "Merry Christmas"......

December 26: A Marine was riding shotgun on our Duster in the TC hatch (the additional opening and seat to the right of the driver) and stood to get a better look and wave at his buddies in the truck in front of us. An enemy sniper's bullet hit him through his left shoulder, the bullet exiting out his right side. The convoy didn't stop. It was The Rough Rider Convoy. The Marine just slumped back into the TC hatch, asleep forever.

I called the turret and automatically slowed the Duster to a crawl and started shooting a slow rate of counter fire at the ridge line all the way to Ca Lu. We didn't tell the two Cannoneers until we got to Ca Lu. They became very upset. We taught them a new phrase: "It's only a thing, you'll get over it. It don't mean nothin'."

*To this day we have never gotten over **IT**.*

December 27: A Marine we called "Chicago", riding on the back of the Duster, got shot through the chest and landed in the turret on top of Earl. Earl kept him breathing and we dropped him off at Ca Lu. Nobody talked about it. I gave Earl a change of shirt, one of our old rag shirts I kept in the side compartment for cleaning the guns. It was better than his blood-soaked one. I was told that the Marine didn't make it. None of us ever knew his real name. Nicknames made it slightly easier for us to accept their fates. We had no words of wisdom for Earl. I just gave him a quick hug, patted his back, and walked away. I lit his blood-stained shirt on fire, but it only smoldered. The glowing embers turned the green jungle fatigue shirt wrinkly black, leaving the blood soaked areas untouched. The last remains of a friend's life…

December 29: We rotated back to Carroll to the ***Water Point*** position. I was hoping to get back on Hill 250 outside the northeast corner of Carroll. Hill 250 had the best view and firing positions, but the Water Point had hot showers and a great field of fire of the western slopes and road leading to Carroll. Plus, it sure beat the river baths with the leeches. Roger Blentlinger, the Marine combat engineer who ran the Water Point, is one of my best Marine friends. He is my personal hero. Every time a Duster or Marine group gets into trouble, he is the first to volunteer for the reactionary team. Roger would always risk his life for our lives. He helped us and several others out of many bad situations.

We started getting ready for a big inspection. The men started joking, "If they inspect our balls, I bet they'll still find crotch rot."

December 30: Roger showed me how he made the water drinkable. He explained to me that the water we got came from either a water truck or through a pipe that was installed from the creek below. The water was then pumped into large rubber vats that were about ten feet round and four feet deep. He then added a few different chemicals. I could not help but think that this was his personal swimming pool and we were getting ready to take a swim. Next, he took a big wooden paddle and walked around each vat, mixing the chemicals and making a whirlpool. After each vat settled, all the bugs and other creatures were in the middle, making it easier for Roger to scoop them out with his net. He then pushed down the edge of the vat to drain off an oily substance floating on top. He said it was the residue left by the planes spraying the area with defoliant called Agent Orange. Finally, the light colored brown water, "ready to drink," was pumped into a big metal water tank that was covered in layers of sandbags. There was only one problem with The Water Point. Every NVA artillery team tried to hit the water tank.

I cannot help but think of the many trips we make to the river, guarding the water tanker trucks as they filled with water. In addition, we have the gruesome job of helping the Marines pull out the dead water buffalos or NVA bodies that blocked the big water pump.

<u>December 31:</u> It is New Year's Eve and they gave our crew the night off. Some of the guys from the motor pool and office had to pull Guard Duty for us. I hoped they knew what they were doing. At 03:00 some Marines, from the Listening Post, were coming through the barbed wire. Dave Woods was the soldier on Guard Duty. The Marines had a password and Dave had a password. When the Marine called out "Geronimo," Dave forgot his response, "Indian", panicked, and started shooting. The Marines were lucky that Dave was nervous and a bad shot. At least, we had a few hours off and no one was injured.

Earl shared with me a note his Mother had placed in his pocket bible.

Hello My Baby,
I thought I could write this better than I could say it. Cause I don't want to cry right now. But remember how much I love you, just look around you and see how big this world is and say to yourself my Mama's heart is just this big and she loves me with every bit of it.
I love you, My Baby.

After I read her note, Earl read out loud the 91st psalm and I prayed I could keep him alive.

James "Doc" Butler

Sgt. Laurier Derosier (on left) with his crew.
Laurier died from the wounds he received on August 30, 1967.

Joe Musso and I celebrating Christmas.

Left to right: Sam Lewis, Joe Belardo, Chester Sines,
David Lewis and Russia Holley.

Earl Holt

Our Duster returned to the ambush site with Lt. Moore
to clear the area of the destroyed trucks.

The booby trapped Marine truck that blew up after we shot it
with a volley of 40mm.

The famous tree we shot that covered Lt. Moore and me with splinters.

Duster at The Rockpile.

*A Duster crew, with a squad of Marines riding on the Duster,
celebrates their safe return through the "Infamous Ambush Alley."*

Lt. Moore's final formation with his platoon.

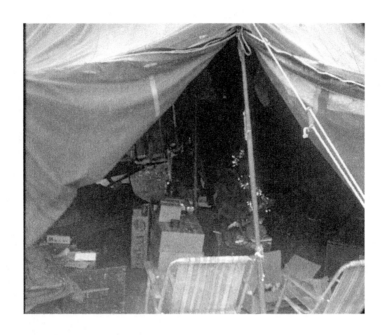

My Christmas tent at The Rockpile.
You can see our Xmas tree decorated with gum wrappers.

Sgt. Cecil Hamilton beat all of us in horseshoes.

Earl Holt (facing forward) waiting for his Christmas dinner.
Check out how dirty his Road Warrior pants are compared
to his friends.

The Camp Carroll mess hall decorated for Christmas.

The cooks did a great job preparing our Christmas meal.

Joe Belardo and Marine Roger Blentlinger.

Here I am checking out the Roger's rubber vat filled with drinking water.

*Shooting at the enemy as they make a daytime assault
towards the Waterpoint and Camp Carroll.*

CHAPTER 7: JANUARY MEANS TET

January 1, 1968: Today is New Year's Day and, at dusk, Tex and I saw what looked like a panther in front of our position. His cry was like the howl of a woman. More than anything, we wanted to be the first to shoot a panther. Grabbing our M-16 and flashlights, we stalked after the animal. Afraid he would end up behind us, we walked somewhat back-to-back, with our flashlights shining down the length of our barrels. Before we could get a shot off, the fast-moving jungle animal disappeared off into the jungle. All we could hear was his cries.

We now have track C142, and it is our job to get it in good running and fighting condition. It is one of the fastest tracks in our section, but still needs to be towed to get it running.

January 2: The crew awoke to find I had replaced the front Duster plate with our old friend "The Grim Reaper."

We trapped eight rats this evening. This beat the old record of five rats and one rat foot! The rats are so big that I had my father send me some muskrat traps. Ordinary rat traps are a joke to these rabbit-sized rodents. The candy, Chuckles, is the best bait. It gives me the creeps when the rats crawl on me. They like to lick my lips and place their nose in my nostrils. I hate the little bastards. I lay there motionless, praying I won't get bit. I don't want to take rabies shots in my belly.

January 3: The Marines issued us a small potbellied stove which we put in our bunker. The monsoon is wet and cold. One day it is 105 degrees hot; the next day it is 40 degrees cold. But, it feels like 20 degrees. I went from wearing tee shirts to long johns and rain gear. The little stove is wonderful. We stole a fuel drip pot from one of the mess hall hot water heaters. We stoked it with rocks and hard teakwood, and let our dripper drip. Five Dustermen and fourteen Marines are warm and dry as toast in our twelve-foot cubical.

January 4: I cannot believe the bullshit; they gave me KP and shit-burning detail again at the main latrine. What a foul way to get rid of human waste! I didn't think I had pissed off anyone lately. It must have been the silly grin and laugh I gave the officers.

We showed them. Tonight, we robbed all the sheet metal and wood the officers had stored for the roof of their new bunker and day room. We used it for our new bunker roof. After we completed our mission, we covered up the new roof with a layer of sandbags to hide our insubordination.

The short break from convoys is a welcome stand down. The only problem with base camp, living at the four-star resort known as Camp Carroll, is the constant ducking to avoid being hit by the NVA artillery.

January 5: We informed our Section Chief, Sgt. Chester Sines, that our telephone land line (lima-lima) that went from the Command Bunker across the camp to our position had been knocked out by the enemy artillery. The lines where strung across the base on telephone poles the Marine Combat Engineers had installed. Since Camp Carroll was always being hit by enemy artillery, the lines could be broken anywhere or in multiple places. We divided up into two, three-man teams. One team started at our bunker and the other started at the Command Bunker, a distance of about 500 yards. After about a two hour search, we found the broken line lying next to one of the poles that crossed over the road where the convoys assemble to leave Camp Carroll. Chester said he knew the supply room had a set of pole climbing spikes, and he would go get them and climb the pole and repair the lines. Like a professional pole climber, Chester ascended the pole. Holding tight to the top, he pulled up one end of the line and reattached it to the pole. As he started to pull up the other end for splicing, we heard the first volley of enemy artillery leave their gun tubes. Screaming, we told Chester to get down.

As the first round landed, we could see that the volley would be heading straight towards Chester. Screaming encouragement, we waited for him to descend. The spikes slipped and Chester fell flat to the pole.

The Last Great Gunfighters

Unable to help him, we were forced to run for our lives as the shells exploded even closer. The five of us huddled in a nearby bunker. Five explosions, ten, twenty, and then came that terrible quiet as we listened for more incoming and people screaming. Sprinting out of the bunker, we feared what we would find. To our surprise, there was Chester, still up on the pole. He was now at the very top, with his arms and legs wrapped tightly around it. We all looked in total amazement. Chester was still alive. There were hundreds of pieces of shrapnel stuck in the pole all around our poor buddy. The pieces ranged in size from only a few inches long to about two feet long. His climbing apparatus and clothes were literally pinned to the pole by the shrapnel. It looked like every square inch of the pole had metal sticking out of it and yet none of it had hit Chester. To get him down, we had to send for the boom truck that was used to install our Duster engines. Straddling the top of the boom, the operator boomed me up to Chester. After what seemed like hours, we had him back on the ground. Chester said that, with each explosion, he could feel the shrapnel hit the pole and shake it violently. All he could do was pray and hold on tight. We are all thankful, amazed and hope we will never have the same experience. God was with Chester today....

January 6: We caught eight rats and killed three scorpions, two centipedes, and one bamboo viper snake. The crew helped replace another engine for one of the other crews. It's amazing how efficient and quick we have become at accomplishing this chore.

I always dream of all kinds of great Italian food, but for some strange reason I keep dreaming of my favorite "Texas Wieners" and promise myself they will be one of my first meals when I get home.

January 7: One of the Marines taught us how to use our track's radio to get in touch with guys from our home states that were also stationed in Nam. Because this was totally illegal to do, we first had to come up with a fictitious name so the CIA could not trace the call back to us. They call it "Radio-Free Nam". I call myself "Jersey Joe". Tonight, I spoke with a guy from Edison, the town next to mine. He called himself "Thomas Edison".

125

January 8:   They called off the "Big Inspection" until the 18th or 19th. Big deal, I am tired of cleaning that hunk of metal. What a joke, inspecting combat teams on the DMZ…

January 13:   We escorted a small convoy of India Company, 3rd Battalion 9th Marines out of Camp J.J. Carroll and headed west on Route 9 with our final destination Ca Lu. Our Duster was rear security. After reaching Ca Lu, we were scheduled to return with another convoy back to Carroll. The convoy was made up of about fifteen Marine trucks and a few Marine tanks. We first stopped at the Khe Gio bridge outpost, dropped off men and supplies, and continued to The Rockpile. At The Rockpile, the convoy regrouped and proceeded to Ca Lu with the remainder of the troops. Our Duster remained as rear security. The Marine mortar ammo truck and a flat bed truck lowboy were positioned in the middle of the convoy.

As the convoy turned into one of the curves in the road, about halfway to Ca Lu (the area known as ***Ambush Alley***), the NVA made their first full-scale attack of the new year. Using command-detonated mines, the NVA blew up the ammo truck and lowboy. Charlie had his shit together and had lined both sides of the road with booby traps and personnel mines. The trucks in front of our Duster came to a scattered halt all over the road. Marines seeking cover started jumping out of and off their vehicles. Landing on personnel mines, they were tossed into the air like rag dolls. It was a terrible sight. It happened in seconds. The NVA soldiers were less than five meters off the road and raked the stalled convoy with automatic weapons, mortars, and RPGs. Our Duster started shooting, but was unable to clear the area close to the convoy because of the mix of NVA and Marines. The Marines, knowing that the land mines and automatic weapons would kill them, were forced to push into the heavy brush and try to regroup. I could see individual and small groups of NVA soldiers moving into the convoy and onto the trucks trying to finish off the survivors and wounded along the road. I shot as many as I could with my M-16 and .45 pistol.

Our Duster's standard shooting and killing routine is to shoot close, sweep quickly out about a 100 yards, mow the middle, start all over, and quickly pick targets. The Marines unconsciously had been drawn into a well-planned ambush. The NVA were shooting RPGs and recoilless rifles from both sides of Route 9. The NVA were so close I could see them throwing satchel charges into the trucks. Our Duster was forced to shoot over the Marines at the NVA shooting from the ridgeline on the north side of the road. Wounded and dead Marines were scattered everywhere. As I drove my Duster slowly forward, I could feel and hear the small NVA personnel mines exploding under my tracks. I feared that the small mines would blow the tracks off, rendering us immobile. Sam Lewis, my squad leader, was screaming in my headset to be careful and not get us killed. We could only advance a few feet before I had to stop and remove the injured and dead Marines from our path. I placed the Marines who were alive on the rear of the Duster. I moved the dead to the side of the road. I felt horrible that I had no time to give them aid. Finally, our 40mm high-explosive shells cleared a path for a group of Marines from the road to the first ridgeline. We positioned the Duster so we could shoot effectively at both the north and south sides of the road. It was important that we suppressed the heavy NVA automatic weapons and RPG teams… or die.

Reinforcements from Ca Lu and the Rockpile were already responding. Our Duster ¾-ton supply truck driver, Spec. 4 John Rowe, a reactionary volunteer from the Rockpile, continually replenished our Duster with ammunition. John and I would first unload the 40mm ammo and then stack his bullet-riddled truck with the wounded from the back of my Duster and the dead off the road. At one point, Rowe was laying between the NVA personnel mines as he emptied his M-16 into the rushing NVA. I lifted him up, dragged him behind the Duster and with a quick burst of my M-16, the landmines exploded. As he pulled into The Rockpile for the third or fourth time, with the last of the wounded we could find, the truck engine seized. The radiator and engine were pierced with bullet holes. Marine reactionary forces from both The Rockpile and Ca Lu saved the day. The Marines regrouped, sweeping both sides of the road, killing and clearing out the NVA.

It was a sad day for "India" Company, 3/9 Marines. We never got to Ca Lu. As we drove back to The Rockpile, our rear deck was covered with Marines, wounded and dead. The Marines had 22 KIA and 60 WIA.

If it weren't for my grenades and another .45 pistol I had acquired from a Marine, I would have been killed today. As I turned to handout more ammo to the guys in the turret, a gook ran up to me and, was so close, I was staring down the length of his rifle barrel. All I heard was a "click". I was lucky, because I think he was out of ammo and I wasn't. Thirteen has become my unlucky, lucky number.

In 1993 at the "Vietnam Women's Memorial" dedication banquet in Washington, D.C., I met former I/3/9 Marine John Lang and he later reintroduced me to Alfred "Flipper" Seals, a survivor of the January 13th battle. That was a day of both tears and joy. They made me an honorary member of their association, "The Flaming I's"...another bond to the Vietnam brotherhood, another toast to the Dusters.

I never understood why we aren't officially allowed to carry side arms. They are confiscated if the Captain finds them. He would have sent me to Leavenworth if he had caught me with all my contraband. We would joke, "Maybe the officers think we will kill someone with a pistol." Wasn't killing the game? I always dreamed of a General driving my Duster and a big NVA Chinese Advisor stepping out in front of the Duster with his AK-47. The old General would be just a little too slow getting his unauthorized .45 pistol out and would catch a bullet smack between the eyes. What a crazy dream, a General driving my Duster!

Back at Carroll, I was running out of shirts to burn. We needed a mail run back to Dong Ha, so we could replenish our clothes from the fatigue rag bin at the motor pool.

Dear Diary:

<u>CRIMSON RED</u>

Nam has four seasons – Living – Learning – Dying – Going Home.

There was a firefight somewhere in Nam. Its exact location could have been anywhere.

Its outcome had been rehearsed a thousand times, as far back as the Crusades.
I could see from my Metal Chariot of Destruction

The Ground Pounders scrambling for cover…
Sniper…Sniper.

I prayed our guns would quell this sniper before his crosshairs found their mark.
Our "Duster's" forty-millimeter cannons blazed as we cleared jungle and tree line.
Like the crack of a whip, a lone shot rang out and one of America's Best flips backwards.

…CRIMSON RED – CRIMSON RED
…CORPSMAN UP – CORPSMAN UP

All guns knew the direction and took aim.
A lone soldier cradles his wounded friend.
…HOLD ON BILLY – HOLD ON
…FOUR HANDS HOLDING – KNUCKLES WHITE
…CRACK – CRACK --- CRACK – CRACK
…HOLD ON, JOHNNY – HOLD ON
…EIGHT HANDS HOLDING – KNUCKLES WHITE

Full auto – Brass a-flying
…A MINUTE DOWN!

Tears now filled this game of death.
A bad omen for America's Best.

Un-heeding the rules of the Dragon's game.
A lone grunt swearing a brother's revenge stood and charged the unseen quest.
...CRACK – CRACK ---- CRACK – CRACK
...CORPSMAN UP – CORPSMAN UP
...CRIMSON POOLS – NOW CRIMSON TIDES
...TWO MINUTES DOWN
...SNIPER GONE
If patience counted, why couldn't he wait?
Now loaded on the back of my "Steel Coffin's" deck.
Standing silently... I apologized for this metal hearse.
...THREE MINUTES DOWN
...AN ETERNITY OF TIME
America's Best withstood another test.

January 14: We returned again to the ambush site looking for a few Marines who were missing. Dead NVA were everywhere. ***What a nightmare!*** The grunts found their missing comrades. I just sucked it up and lit another Tareyton.

January 15: We finally finished recovering all the Marines and equipment from the battle. I have not received mail from home in four days. It is very unusual for them not to write or send a CARE package.

January 16: Still being on someone's shit list, I had KP again. But it sure felt good to get off The Road and get a hot meal.

January 17: The Seabees got hit. Four were wounded. They were working a little past the Sand-Gravel Pit. Now we had to clean up Seabee blood. "God, how much more do you want us to endure?"

January 18: We passed that BIG inspection. The only thing that we accomplished by having that inspection was that all the Dusters got a good cleaning and the area was policed.

January 19: I received a letter from my Mom telling me all about Christmas. She was going to save my presents for me to open when I get home, ***if I get home***. In her letters, Mom loved to tell me about everything they ate—daily and holidays. She didn't know that we were starving, and I couldn't tell her. I would read her letters to the crew. "We had the freshest Italian bread, the best tossed salad, cold antipasto with everything you like: salami, pepperoni, prosciutto, provolone, olives, artichoke hearts, roasted red peppers plus the seven fishes of Christmas, baked ham, Dad's homemade lasagna, wine and all kinds of dessert from Bovella's Bakery." Our mouths drooled as I read her letters. I then began our time-honored tradition of opening my switchblade and slicing every description of food from my Mom's letter. The guys held out their hands as I filled their palms with the equally shared pieces of paper food. We tossed them into our mouths, a course at a time, moaning in ecstasy and laughing hysterically as we savored the paper meals from home. Dessert was the highlight of our gourmet meal, eating Bovella's famous almond cookies and rum cakes. It was a meal fit for any Warrior King.

January 20: The "B" Battery convoy got hit below Carroll, and suffered two WIA. At 1300 hours, Carroll got hit with another 74 NVA rockets. At 1630 hours, our Duster spotted the smoke from the NVA rocket tube shooting at Carroll. We dueled with the NVA as their rockets burst all around us. The crew cheered when we saw the first enemy secondary explosion, proof of our day's kill. I bitched because it took one hundred sixty-five 40mm rounds to finish off the gook rocket team. ***Thank God the NVA only shot one rocket at a time.*** My crew knew I wouldn't put up with them missing their target, any target. It made me crazy.

January 21: At sunup, the base got hit with more **"INCOMING!"** Earl saw a wisp of smoke coming out of the lower tree line along Dong Ha Mountain and yelled that he could see the location of the Gooks' artillery. Because Holley, our Gunner, was on KP, we told Earl that, since he was trained on Dusters, he could get himself a few kills. The enemy guns were about a mile away and in range of our 40s. I stood behind the turret and gave Earl some words of encouragement before he pressed the trigger. Sam Lewis, traversing the turret, told Earl he was on target and to shoot the first round high and adjust on target. It took less than ten seconds after the first round exploded for Earl to put our next volley on top of the Gooks' heads. With a quick 120 rounds, we made our square with an "X" in the middle, and the Gooks were eliminated. We all cheered as we got three secondary explosions. We peppered the area with another 40 rounds, just to make sure nobody escaped.

Later this afternoon, the Marine search team told Earl he had seven confirmed kills. By this evening, Earl became very withdrawn and sad. I had a long conversation with him, trying to explain to him that he would be okay. "Joe, I just killed seven men. Even though we consider them the enemy, it was seven men with families. How do I sort this? How will God forgive me? How do you do it?" I did not have a real answer for my friend. "Earl, you'll just get used to it." As I walked away, I could see the tears flowing down his cheeks and I remembered how much it hurts. ***How could I explain to him that it's probably only going to get worse?***

January 22: At 1800 hours, the NVA hit the base by the 175mm cannon area with four shells, wounding soldiers from the 2nd Battalion 94th Artillery.

January 23: We saw three NVA in front of our position and fired at them. Later, we only found traces of blood and some parts. I'm sure I nailed one in the chest. We blamed the Marines for shooting without authorization.

Marines

Route 9 – Ambush Alley

Route 9 – further on Ambush Alley.

Route 9 – Ambush Alley escort duty.

Hand grenade being thrown during a fire fight.

Wounded

John Rowe

Two carrying one

CHAPTER 8: THE MOTHER OF ALL BATTLES

January 24, 1968: We got involved in a large ambush below Camp J.J. Carroll on Route 9. This battle had the fury of a tornado.

Without our knowledge, we ended up fighting against the combined enemy forces of the 320th Infantry Division, the 48th and 52nd Regiments. Being outnumbered and overrun took on a whole new meaning. These events were so remarkable that this battle has entered the annals of military history and comprised the stories featured in LTC Ollie North's program "Men At War" on Fox TV.

THE OFFICIAL MILITARY HISTORIC THIRD PERSON ACCOUNT:

Taken from the After Action Report, Fort Bliss, TX; and from the ADA (Air Defense Artillery Magazine) #HQDA 44-96-2, March-April 1996.

0700 hours: Section Chief SGT Sines had accompanied one of his section's tracks to the Camp Carroll Battery "C" maintenance motor pool for repair. The normal crew of the track consisted of Squad Leader SGT Sam Lewis, Gunner SP4 Russia Holley, Cannoneers SP4 Earl Holt and PFC David Lewis, and Driver SP4 Joseph Belardo. At the motor pool, the crew was to replace both 40mm cannons with new barrels; repair damaged track treads; and replace the starter, since the current way to start the track was by pulling it with another track. After a few hours, the track treads were repaired and re-tensioned; the engine oiled and checked; and both barrels were replaced, but not fully cleaned. The starter was not yet replaced or repaired. In the distance the crew could hear what sounded like a full-scale firefight, a common sound along the DMZ.

1130 hours: A two-and-a-half-ton truck traveling from Camp Carroll to Cam Lo on Route 9 received small-arms fire. The Army vehicle following the truck received mortar fire as well as small-arms fire. The occupants of both vehicles, upon reaching Cam Lo, warned a convoy pulling out of Cam Lo for Camp Carroll that Route 9 had been interdicted. The Marine Captain in charge of the convoy disregarded the warning. Being shot at on Route 9 west of Cam Lo was a common everyday occurrence. As the convoy approached a small bridge that crossed a minor tributary of the Cam Lo River, the NVA regulars hidden in the hills overlooking Route 9 ambushed the convoy with small arms, automatic weapons, recoilless rifles, rocket-propelled grenades (RPGs) and mortars. The overwhelmed convoy was halted in minutes by the NVA. The troops were shocked by the intensity of the firefight and incoming rounds. Those still alive were forced to take cover along the edge of the road.

1135 hours: The observation post on Hill 250 outside the northeast corner of Camp Carroll (the 4th Marine Regiment's combat base and home of "C" Charlie Battery, 1st Battalion, 44th Artillery "Dusters") noticed explosions along Route 9. Large numbers of enemy were observed moving along the river and ridgelines north of the ambush site. The Dustermen and Marines manning the outpost (OP) were now aware that an ambush was taking place in front of Camp Carroll. They could see NVA infantry crossing the Cam Lo River in boats. Explosions and smoke were coming from the ambushed convoy. The OP requested permission to fire their Duster at the enemy, and the 4th Marines granted their request. Simultaneously, Camp Carroll was advised that the convoy was being ambushed and prepared for a possible assault on Camp Carroll.

The camp forces were advised that the fight was just below the eastern slope of Camp Carroll. All Dusters in the battery area were instructed to take positions along the northern camp perimeter. All other tracks were to hold position and await instructions. SGT Lewis' track was one of five Dusters that began to shoot more than 8,000 40mm rounds at the NVA that had attacked the convoy on Route 9 in the valley in front of Carroll. Lt. Hardin had taken command of one of the Dusters, comprised of a new inexperienced crew. The only seasoned combat veteran was squad leader Johnny Towns, who had only one week left to DEROS (going home). Towns' crew consisted of Gunner SP4 Jackie Gilbert, Cannoneers PFC Shora Solomon, PFC Townsend, and Driver

SP4 Robert Conley. Lt. Hardin instructed Lewis to saddle up, refuel, replenish ammo and meet his Duster within fifteen minutes at the camp gate as a reaction force for the ambushed convoy. Lewis instructed Lt. Hardin of the Duster's starting problem, but was still ordered to follow, since Hardin needed a seasoned fighting crew. Lewis instructed his crew to return to their position "water point" and re-supply. The crew hastily fueled, ringed the turret with 40mm ammo, restocked upper and side turret ammo compartments, and filled the Driver's compartment with all the extra reserve of loose clips of 40mm ammo. Section chief SGT-E6, Chester Sines went as the extra sixth combatant and sat to the right of the driver in the extra hatch known as the "TC" seat.

1200 hours: The two Dusters met two Marine tanks and a squad of Marines at the main gate. A Marine LT was in command of the first M48 Tank and was followed out the gate by Lt. Hardin's Duster; next in line was the other M48 tank with half the Marine squad holding on to that tank; and then by Lewis's Duster along with the balance of the Marines sitting on the back of the Duster. The relief force stopped within 100 yards of the ambushed convoy and began to give direct fire to enemy forces along the northern ridge above the convoy. Via radio, Joe Belardo instructed the Driver of the other Duster, SP4 Conley, via radio to keep a fighting distance between his Duster and the M48 tank in front of him and the ambush site. All was now relatively quiet at the ambush sight. Americans could be seen lying in the kill zone, wounded or dead. There was no shooting now from the NVA or the convoy. The only sound was the eerie whistle of hundreds of Duster 40mm shells from Camp Carroll shooting over their heads and exploding into the slopes along Dong Ha Mountain.

Both lieutenants instructed all tracks to proceed forward with caution into the ambush site. Belardo instructed Conley to hold fast and not move. Sines advised both lieutenants that this was not a hit-and-run NVA action, and that all caution should be used and not to advance. Sines advised them to sweep both the north and south sides of the convoy before moving forward. SP4 Belardo advised Conley to drive the Duster to his right and take position on a small, elevated knoll overlooking the convoy so they could get a better look at the situation. Sines advised Hardin to reassess the situation and to clear the area around the convoy before advancing into a possible trap.

Seeing no NVA, both officers again instructed their drivers to proceed slowly and cautiously along the center of the road. SGT Lewis instructed his Duster and the other M48 to hold fast and be ready to fire. The first M48 Tank had just crossed over the small bridge that spanned a small creek on Route 9. Lt. Hardin's Duster was just approaching the bridge. Both tracks had traveled no more than 100 yards. The NVA, hidden from view, suddenly ambushed the M48 and Duster with volleys of RPGs and satchel charges. Both tracks were instantly out of action. The crew of the M48 were all either seriously wounded or killed. The crew on Lt. Hardin's Duster had four men with minor wounds and two seriously wounded. Squad Leader Towns could be seen standing in the burning Duster turret, shooting the M60 machine gun at the rushing enemy soldiers. Cannoneer Solomon had lost the back of his legs from one of the RPGs. Gunner SP4 Gilbert had lost both his arms from another RPG.

Squad Leader Lewis' Duster immediately opened fire on the RPG teams, killing the first four RPG teams they could see. Caution had to be taken because the remaining RPG teams were within feet of the destroyed M48 and Duster. SP4 Belardo instructed the driver of the other M48 Tank to follow him and take position on that small knoll overlooking the ambush site. Both tracks did figure eights to level any tall grass that would conceal the enemy and to give an area for the squad of Marines to dig in. As they drove up the knoll they were firing at the NVA that were visible and instructed the twelve Marines that came with them to dig in and protect the west and south slopes of the knoll.

1315 hours: Lewis' Duster and the other M48 were now about 100 yards off the road on the south side of Route 9. The ambushed convoy along with the other destroyed Duster and M48 were 150 to 200 yards slightly to the right, at their one o'clock position. Lewis' field of fire was excellent. The terrain around the knoll was mostly low brush and grass. Directly across Route 9 was an area about 200 to 300 yards wide that went north for about one-quarter mile to a small hedgerow along the Cam Lo River. The area was clear and had small clusters of brush. The small stream at the ambush site ran back north to the river. Its eastern side terrain was hilly and covered with heavy brush. This area was known as Mike Hill because the Marines had lost many men from Mike Company on the hills in a previous battle. The south side of the bridge had similar terrain. At the bridge crossing stood a lone tree about seventy feet tall, later to be known as Ground Zero. The destroyed Duster was in close proximity to the tall tree. At the eleven o'clock position in front of Lewis' Duster was the beginning of a large hill with heavy cover and a steep drop-off. The area behind Lewis' Duster was a sharp steady rise up to Camp Carroll and the Observation Post known as Hill 250.

1330 hours: Sines requested reinforcements from Camp Carroll. Captain Easter, "C" Battery 1st/44th Commanding Officer, advised: "Hold position, recover men, casualties and equipment from ambush, return to Camp Carroll." Lewis' Duster proceeded slowly towards the entrapped destroyed Duster and tank, raking the area with 40mm and M60 machine gun fire. SP4 Belardo repeatedly tried to contact the destroyed tracks via radio, but now only received radio microphone clicking. The other M48 gave rear security as the Marines hastily dug new positions. Lewis' Duster was now within 50 yards of the destroyed Duster. NVA automatic weapons and machine guns now opened fire. RPGs from across Route 9 were fired, falling short of their mark or soaring overhead. A small group of NVA began to rush forward, only to be killed by 40mm fire. NVA 57mm recoilless rifles began shooting at the Duster from the eleven o'clock position. More NVA started rushing from concealed positions along the road. SGT Chester Sines instructed Belardo to return back up the knoll. Belardo was unwilling to turn around and expose the Duster's sides or the engine, fearing a RPG or 57 recoilless hit would destroy the Duster. Holt used inter-track radio communications to verbally guide him backwards and up the hill until they were sure that turning was safe.

Automatic weapons fire was constantly strafing the Duster, and mortars were exploding at close range. Sines again radioed Camp Carroll advising enemy action and requesting backup. Carroll advised him to hold position and sweep the area. The new 40mm cannon barrels, recently installed at Carroll, had not been completely cleaned and began to smoke profusely from the cosmoline oil. The Duster stopped shooting as Belardo and Holt feverishly swabbed the barrels with the little reserve oil left on the Duster. NVA could be seen running out in the open along the small stream and into the heavy brush at the eleven o'clock position, and along the stream that headed towards the ambush site. The Duster again began firing along the stream area, delivering effective fire on the advancing NVA. Large groups of NVA, dead and wounded, were now visible from the river to within 20 yards of the ambushed convoy. NVA mortars once more began landing in the Duster area. NVA automatic weapons and small arms fire were sporadic but heavy. SP4 Belardo was advised to keep his track moving around the knoll and away from the Marine infantry and M48. A moving target was not as easy a target.

The M48 took up position by the path that was made by the two tracks as they went up the knoll. The Marines dug in slightly to the left and rear of the M48. Sines, the sixth man of normally a five man crew, now stood on the back of the Duster giving firing orders, exposing him to enemy fire. Belardo began giving artillery coordinates to the Fire Direction Control at Carroll. The enemy could now be seen dragging their dead or wounded into the heavy brush. Sines, now as the driver, and Belardo in the TC hatch, advanced the Duster towards the destroyed convoy, raking the area with 40mm and M60 fire. The NVA again charged the Duster. Sines stopped the Duster and was holding position. The Duster was now only a few yards from Route 9 and less than 30 yards from the destroyed Duster. The Duster was now shooting direct fire at the charging NVA. Belardo, exposing himself to enemy fire, now stood on the top front right corner of the Duster so he could see the other Duster. Only gunner Gilbert's head was visible and not moving. No other Duster crewmen could be seen.

Sines was now shooting Belardo's M-16 at the advancing NVA from the Driver's compartment. Belardo, now on the ground outside the Duster, had the front main door of the Duster open. This was a common combat practice for Duster Drivers. It was the only way to take the 40mm ammo out of the inside storage area and hand it to the loaders in the turret. Belardo, continually exposing himself to enemy fire, repeatedly climbed in and out of the Driver's hatch, retrieving 40mm ammo and distributing it to the loaders in the turret. Belardo advised Sines that the 40mm ammo was extremely low. NVA RPGs, mortars and 57mm recoilless rifles began hitting close to the Duster. Belardo was instructed by Sines to get back in the Duster as they did a 180-degree turn, and headed back up the knoll. Two helicopters, that had been called to help, began shooting extremely close to the east slope of the Duster and advised them that a very large NVA force had crossed over Route 9 and was advancing towards them from the east and up to Camp Carroll. The helicopters continued to shoot into a small ravine that headed up to Camp Carroll and covered the eastern slope of the knoll. The M48 was now out of 40mm ammo, so its crew began using their rifles. Sitting motionless, the NVA stopped shooting at the M48 with mortars and RPGs, possibly thinking they had already scored a direct hit. The dug-in Marines, almost out of ammo, were using reserve M-16 ammo borrowed from the Duster.

1415 hours: Belardo radioed Carroll that the 40mm ammo was down to 60 rounds and they would not abandon the convoy, expected to be overrun, needed ammo and reinforcements immediately. Jets had now arrived and were dropping bombs and napalm on the north side of the river. The Duster continued to shoot the M60 machine gun at the visible NVA. Sines and Belardo continued to direct air strikes and napalm strikes on the NVA positions. The NVA had now stopped shooting at the Duster. Out of nowhere, a small group of villagers began running across the open combat field between Route 9 and the river, heading west towards Cam Lo. After they disappeared, no other shots were fired from either side. The NVA seemed to vanish. Maybe they were digging-in, out of view in the heavy cover, or trying to avoid the jet air strikes. Camp Carroll had stopped shooting 40mm and heavy artillery fearing it would hit the helicopters or jets. Sines again radioed Carroll reminding them of the situation and that forty to fifty NVA laid dead on the knoll next to the Duster, and what seemed to be hundreds of NVA lay dead between Route 9 and the river. NVA could now be seen dragging their wounded into heavy cover.

Sines repeated that they needed ammo and reinforcements and would not give up the hill advantage to the NVA. Captain Easter advised that no reinforcements were coming, but a small group of volunteers would try to bring ammo and that the Duster should hold position until they arrived. SP4 Robert Williams was the ammo truck driver along with Duster crewman SP4 Donald Wolfe and four other volunteers. Fearing the ammo truck would run into the NVA and hoping to intercept it before it reached the ambush site, Belardo proceeded alone down the west slope of the knoll to Route 9 about 100 yards from the Duster, on the same path they drove up to get on the knoll. It was the Duster crew's belief that if Belardo reached the ammo truck, he could direct it back up the knoll after which the Duster could replenish its ammo, extract the wounded and dead from the ambush, and return to Carroll. The Marines had been instructed to keep this path open, knowing it was the alternate route back to Route 9 and Camp Carroll. Belardo, armed with M-16 and hand grenades, sprinted down the knoll through the dead NVA, shooting into the heavy brush killing any NVA in his path and throwing grenades at enemy positions. The Marines constantly gave support fire. At the road, Belardo waited and crouched in a drainage ditch. NVA could be seen taking up position across the road. Belardo quickly dispatched six of the NVA he could see and threw the remaining grenades into other NVA positions across Route 9. Belardo, waiting for the ammo truck, could hear automatic weapons fire and explosions from the west on Route 9 in the direction of the ammo truck. The ammo truck was being riddled with NVA automatic weapons fire, wounding Wolfe. Twenty minutes had elapsed and no ammo truck arrived. Belardo began his return back up the knoll, shooting at the enemy from behind the dead NVA bodies as he advanced up the hill.

1500 hours: The Duster crew radioed Carroll that they were almost completely out of ammunition. Carroll advised that they had dispatched a second group of volunteers with a Marine weapons squad. Belardo, in contact with the second ammo truck via radio, advised SP4 John Huelsenbeck and Marine CPL Roger Blentlinger, a combat engineer and volunteer weapons man aboard the ammo truck, as to the road area where he would meet them. Belardo again descended down the hill. The Marines and Duster were not giving support fire because ammunition was very low. They now could see Belardo about halfway down the slope engaging NVA soldiers in hand-to-hand combat. Quickly overcoming and dispatching the enemy, Belardo continued to fight his way down to the road. At Route 9, Belardo now wounded from an enemy bayonet hastily moved west and waved down the second ammo truck with its reinforcements. Belardo, riding on the running board of the ammo truck, directed it and one other truck with about twelve Marines, up the path. About fifty yards up the hill, the ammo truck slid off the path and its front wheel fell into a ditch and was unable to move. The other Marine truck was unable to push it out. Mortars began landing all around the two trucks. Huelsenbeck ordered the Marine officer on the other truck to move his vehicle and have his men dig in and give support fire. Huelsenbeck, exposing himself to enemy fire, positioned the Marines for maximum support. Belardo was now running up the hill through the enemy mortar barrage and heavy automatic weapons fire to get to the Duster. The Duster was now proceeding down the eastern slope of the knoll spraying the ravine that led to Carroll with M60 gunfire. The jets and helicopters had left the area. A lone observation plane could be seen flying on the eastern side of the stream.

Belardo advised the crew what had happened and drove the Duster to the stranded ammo truck. At the ammo truck Holt, using the M60, gave additional fire support for Huelsenbeck and Blentlinger. Exposing themselves to enemy fire, they fastened the Duster tow cable to the ammo truck. The ammo truck, laden with ammunition, was pulled to the top of the knoll. The Marine lieutenant was now assessing the situation with SGT Sines. The officer, after viewing the battle area from on top the Duster, agreed to try to secure the path back to Route 9. The ammo truck was now parked behind the Duster's right south side. As the reactionary crew replenished the Marines and Duster with M-16, M60 ammo, and a truckload of 40mm ammo, the Duster crew again opened fire on the advancing NVA. The crew, giving each other a needed rest, took on new assignments. Squad Leader Sam Lewis was now the Gunner, seated in the turret on the left side of the twin 40mm cannons. Belardo, behind him as Cannon Loader, stood on the left side of the 40mm cannons. Traversing the turret was SP4 Russia Holly. Holt was behind him as the other Cannon Loader. PFC Dave Lewis, now standing on the outside of the turret, shot the M60. Huelsenbeck and Blentlinger were handing Belardo and Holt 40 mm ammo. A human assembly line was humping shells from the ammo truck to the Duster.

The Duster, now shooting on full auto, first cleared the ravine leading to Carroll and shot as close to the destroyed convoy as possible. The NVA again opened fire with mortars and 57mm recoilless rifles, and again could be seen crossing the river in large groups. Sines, on the ground with another group, was reloading the inside of the Duster with 40mm and giving artillery coordinates to Carroll's FDC. The ammo team was yelling to the crew in the turret, giving them additional NVA 57mm recoilless rifle and mortar targets they could see. Secondary explosions were everywhere. The Duster crew and the NVA were not giving ground. Killing the NVA was again at an all-time high. When fully loaded, the Duster along with the Marines were going to clear a path to the ambushed convoy, rescue the dead and wounded, destroy the damaged vehicles and return to Carroll. The crew had now fired an additional 2,000 40mm rounds. The 40mm cannons, red-hot, began to jam and cook-off without firing. Holt and Belardo repeatedly reached into the cannon breeches with their bare hands to remove the hot 40mm rounds before they self-exploded. The twin 40s now had two 40mm shells jammed half in the breech, not allowing the firing block to move into firing position. Holt stepped out of the turret, hoping to find more oil on the ammo truck or Marine truck. The oil would be used to free the overheated cannon breeches. Belardo continued to reach in the hot breech trying to dislodge the jammed shells. NVA artillery rocked the Duster and ammo truck.

Squad Leader Lewis, seeing a NVA team shoot a 57 recoilless rifle, yelled, "Duck!" The 57s hit the ground a few feet from the Duster. The explosions threw Holt, Huelsenbeck, and Blentlinger over the ammo truck. PFC Dave Lewis was hit in the face with shrapnel and stood frozen with blood running into his eyes and down his face. Two more NVA shells hit the area, the explosions tossing David Lewis between the Duster and ammo truck. Squad Leader Sam Lewis, with bad head wounds, lay unconscious or possibly dead in the Gunner's seat. Belardo was now on his back lying over the 40mm cannon breeches with head, chest and arm wounds. The two 40mm rounds in the breech exploded, wounding Belardo a second time and sending him up and on top of Sam Lewis. Holly, who was sitting on the other side of the turret, was thrown unconscious but unwounded, on top of Dave Lewis between the Duster and the ammo truck. Belardo, still conscious and covered in blood, thought the Duster had been hit a second or third time. The turret was now in flames and filled with smoke. Belardo, seeing Sam Lewis unconscious and bleeding, picked him out of the Gunner's seat Belardo, with Lewis on his shoulder and armed with an M-16 from the turret, held onto the hot 40mm barrels and exited the Duster. Belardo, carrying Lewis and firing the M-16 at the advancing NVA, moved behind the ammo truck.

The event happened so quickly that the Marines by the M48 were now just responding with aid and counter fire. The ammo crew was trying to assess damage and regroup. Duster medic James "Doc" Butler, who was one of the reactionary volunteers, was quickly giving medical aid to the wounded. Belardo, refusing medical aid, climbed back into the turret and used the fire extinguisher on the burning cannons. Grabbing the M60 from its mount, Belardo returned fire, killing the advancing NVA. Huelsenbeck, Holt and Blentlinger joined Belardo in the turret. Holt and Huelsenbeck frantically tried to salvage the cannons and clear the loading magazines of hot 40mm ammo. Unable to fix the cannons, they commandeered M-16 and remained up in the turret giving direct fire at the rushing NVA. The survivors held on, hoping to get relief from a reactionary force.

CHAPTER 9: RESCUE FROM DONG HA

January 24, 1968 at 1600 hours: While this battle raged, Capt. V. J. Tedesco, the 1/44 Artillery liaison officer, was in the Officer's Club at Dong Ha enjoying a cold beer, totally unaware that one of his combat batteries was in a hellacious firefight. Word came from Lieutenant Colonel John House, the Battalion Commander that Charlie Battery and some Marines were in deep contact with the NVA on Route 9 and needed some serious bailing out or would be overrun. As the liaison officer, it wasn't Tedesco's job to take out the Dong Ha reaction force, but the Reaction Force Commander couldn't be located.

1700 hours: Sines advised Carroll of the situation and told them he would try to get back to Carroll. The wounded Duster men and Marines were placed inside the M48 and in the Duster TC hatch. With Marines lying on the top decks of the Duster, M48, and loaded into the trucks, they departed the knoll. Sines drove the Duster with Belardo at the M60. Huelsenbeck, Holt and Blentlinger were shooting their M-16 and throwing grenades. With the two trucks in the middle and the M48 bringing up the rear, they blasted their way through enemy positions and fought their way up Route 9 and back to Camp Carroll.

At Carroll they were advised by Captain Easter to keep the chatter down about all the NVA in the valley. Easter did not want the men to think that Carroll could or would be overrun. The crew was ordered back to the water point position to stand guard duty. The wounded were medivaced to Dong Ha and Da Nang. Sines and his crew were never again asked about the ambush, although their heroic actions were probably the reason Camp JJ Carroll was not overrun.

1730 hours: Tedesco led two Dusters and two truck-mounted Quad-50s to the rescue. The following morning, he described the action in a tape made for his wife, Suzanne. "I don't know where to start to tell you, Suzanne, about what happened yesterday, well last night, to be exact," Tedesco said. "I guess I'll start from the beginning. I was over in the club around a quarter to five when we got word that Charlie

Battery was in contact with the enemy on Route 9 between Cam Lo and Camp Carroll. They had gone to try to relieve a convoy that had been ambushed on that road, and they were in deep contact. They needed help and Rick Taylor wasn't around. He is the Reaction Force Commander; I'm the alternate commander. Rick wasn't around, so it was my job to take the reaction force in there and try to bail Charlie Battery out."

"We left Dong Ha about 5:30, or 1730, and it took us a half hour to get out to the ambush site," he continued. "I had with me two Dusters and two Quads. I was in the lead Duster, the Quads were in the middle, and there was one Duster in back. When we approached the ambush site, I saw a tank off to the side of the road. Apparently knocked out of action; it was abandoned. Later, I found dead lying on the front deck of the tank. There were four trucks and a jeep in the convoy, lined up straight down the middle of the road. Every one of them had been knocked out. The jeep had been knocked out by an RPG, which is similar to our bazooka or 3.5-rocket launcher. The people from the convoy were hiding against the vehicles and against the sides of the road; not doing anything very much, but looking very horrible and scared and frightened. I saw, farther up the road and across a little bridge, Charlie Battery's Duster off to the side of the road. The guns pointed crazily up at the sky, the hatch in front was open, and nobody was visible around the track. I took my track, and we drove past the tank and pulled off the side of the road and proceeded toward Charlie Battery's track to find out what the story was with them and to give them any support we could."

"As we started moving along the road," Tedesco continued, "we had to pull way off the road into the bushes because there were so many wounded all along the side of the road. We moved back on the road and across the bridge, and I moved my track off the road to my right and saw where the fire was coming from. We were receiving sniper fire, and the Air Force was putting air strikes into the area."

Tedesco directed the track commander, SGT Vincent DeSantis, to return the fire raking the column. With DeSantis directing fire and loading the guns, the Duster delivered effective fire against the NVA automatic weapons, recoilless rifle, and mortar positions in the surrounding hills.

Tedesco left the track and ran across the road to Charlie Battery's track, looking for the officer or NCO in charge, hoping to find out what had happened. He found Lt. Hardin and discovered three of Lt. Hardin's five-man crew had been wounded when RPGs had slammed into their track. SP4 Gilbert in the turret had had both arms blown off by the first RPG. The second RPG had wounded the gunner, PVT Solomon. The explosion had ripped the muscles, tendons and flesh from the back of his legs. Then, the track had taken two more RPG hits in quick succession. Marines who had been riding on Lt. Hardin's track were also wounded. Nearby, a Marine lieutenant, who could not speak because his lower jaw had been shot away, was calmly writing down grid coordinates on a piece of paper. He passed the piece of paper to his radio operator, who tried to call in fire missions; not knowing his radio was broken.

Running in a low crouch across the road, Tedesco re-crossed the bridge and made his way past the main body of the convoy, past the knocked-out tank to where he had left the two Bravo Battery Quad-50s and rear Duster. He directed their fire on the hills on either side of the road at the same place the Marines were placing their fire and where the sniper fire was coming from. Satisfied the rounds were on target, he moved back down the line, trying to find the officer in command of the convoy.

"There were two officers, a Marine Captain and an Army Lieutenant present," Tedesco said. "All they could do was hide up against the track. There were wounded all over the place. Suzanne, it was horrible. People were dead and wounded all over the place. The wounded were in a complete state of shock. It was almost impossible to get them to move off the road, set up some security and try to get the convoy functioning. Anyway, when I saw that these two officers weren't very willing or capable of taking command, I took command of the entire convoy. And my first problem was trying to get the wounded out. We got on the horn and notified Carroll what the situation was, the fact that we needed infantry security and needed aircraft in to evacuate the wounded."

While Tedesco was busy trying to reorganize the convoy, the NVA concentrated their fire on Bravo's lead Duster. Seriously wounded in the back, De Santis refused medical aid and continued to direct his crew's fire and load the guns. Then, an RPG struck the rear of the turret, killing one of the Cannoneers and wounding the rest of the crew. Wounded a second time, DeSantis continued to refuse medical aid and, with bullets showering all around him, began evacuating the casualties from the stricken vehicle.

"I moved back down the road across the bridge and headed to my track to try to find out what was going on," said Tedesco, "and I noticed that my track - the track I had come in on - was not firing," he continued. "As I crossed the bridge, someone called to me from the bushes on the bank of the little stream the bridge goes over. And it was the sergeant [DeSantis] who had been aboard the track. He had taken a small arm sniper round in his back and fragments in his arm. Two of the other three people who had been in the tub with the sergeant were both wounded and in the bushes with him. We didn't know where the fourth man who had been up in the tub was at the time. We later found out that the Cannoneer killed was SP4 Billy Strickland."

"The sergeant told me that they had been hit again," Tedesco continued. "I ran around to the front of the track to try to get to the radio to let them know we had lost another track, and I saw a horrible, horrible sight. The driver, the man who had driven me in there, had apparently been sitting with his head out of the hatch when an RPG or an aerial bomb, I'm not sure which one it was, landed near the track: and it just blew shrapnel and debris all over his face and shoulders and neck. I thought the man was dead. As of now, he's still alive. He's still in critical condition, but they think he might pull through now. The radio was out of action and everything was covered with blood. I moved across the road back to Hardin's track again, trying to get medical aid for the guy in the track, in case he was still alive, and for the sergeant and his people."

"Meanwhile, all of this time I ran across more and more wounded, more and more dead, and more and more scattered groups of Marines. I was trying to organize them, trying to move them," he continued. "We had a medivac chopper come in, and we started taking small arms fire all over the place. I ran over to the chopper and got him out of the area before he got downed right in the middle of our area, so we'd never get anything in or out. This went on and on and on, Suzanne, just on and on and on. I kept moving up and down the convoy, kept calling for the infantry. I kept calling for the artillery. As it started getting darker, I kept calling for illumination."

The illumination rounds, bursting high overhead, released parachute flares that bathed the terrain in an eerie orange glow. Tedesco knew the NVA might use the cover of darkness to move in for the kill.

"Finally," he continued, "I decided we were going to load all the wounded on the two Quad-50s, and on the Dusters and make a run for it. Well, we had gotten one of the Quads loaded with wounded when two Seabee trucks came in to help us on their own; and we got the dead and some more wounded loaded. All of a sudden, the choppers started coming in. The choppers started landing all around us, taking out the wounded."

"Now that the wounded were going," Tedesco said, "my main concern was my two tracks that were out of action. I moved back across the bridge. There were at least 50 civilians in the area. I had no idea where they came from. We had fired over their heads to keep them down. We weren't sure whether they were VC – NVA, or what they were doing. We had a Marine sergeant covering them the whole time with a machine gun. We finally got some trucks in and got the wounded moving out on the trucks, and then the helicopters came in and we kept evacuating. We started pulling back toward the main convoy, evacuating all the wounded with us, picking up all the weapons. I left Lieutenant Gregg, one of the officers from Bravo Battery, in charge there, and he saw to it that the wounded were medivaced."

"Lt. Hardin and I returned with a bunch of Marines to secure our Dusters. This was my main concern now. What were we going to do with the Dusters? I didn't want to leave them to the enemy. I requested permission to destroy the Dusters, and battalion denied this permission. They said another relief column was on their way."

A third reaction force commanded by Captain Charlie Vickers, the 1/44 Artillery S-4, roared out of Dong Ha. The reaction force consisted of 1/44 personnel acting as infantry, two Dusters from A/1-44, two Quad -50s from G/65, and four ammunition-laden five-ton trucks from 1/ 44, Headquarters Battery. They reached the ambush site at 1900 hours.

"Well, about 7 o'clock, or 1900, it was getting pretty dark, and I was just about to say "to hell with battalion" and blow them [the Dusters] anyway, when I saw the headlights of the Charlie Vicker's relief column. Once Charlie got there with his extra force and his people, things cleared up pretty quickly. We got the rest of the wounded out and as many of the dead as we could get out. Lt. Hardin started my original track and found it could run, and he drove that out. Charlie brought one of his tracks across the bridge and hooked the Charlie Battery track (Lt. Hardin's original track) up with the tow cable, and we towed that out. Charlie covered my withdrawal with one of his Dusters that were still operational. And finally at 1930, or 7:30, we left the ambush site.

"We moved out to Cam Lo at the district headquarters there," Tedesco said. "There we left the vehicles that weren't operative and, with the help of the Huey gunships, we came the rest of the way back into Dong Ha. We got back to Dong Ha about 10 o'clock, or 2200 hours. It was a very, very horrible -unbelievably horrible - experience. I don't guess I will ever forget the sight of that battlefield, or the look on the face of that poor kid who was driving me after I got back to the track and found that they had been hit. I didn't sleep very much. In fact, I didn't sleep at all last night." The 3rd Battalion, 4th Marines Regiment moved in to secure the ambush site, standing watch through the night over the dead and disabled vehicles.

Following the ambush, the survivors discovered that they had gone up against elements of the NVA's 320th Division's 48th and 52nd Regiment. Total friendly casualties were seventeen killed in action, 42 wounded seriously enough to require medical evacuation, and 13 with minor wounds. The 1/ 44th artillery had committed 11 Dusters, five Quad-50s and 152 soldiers. They had fired over 20,000 40mm shells and 28,000 .50-caliber rounds. The ambush was supported by direct and indirect field artillery, jets and Huey gun-ships. Captain Tedesco, Lt. Hardin and SGT DeSantis were awarded the Silver Star.

After the battle, the Marines placed a dead NVA atop a mile marker adjacent to the ambush site, and then added a helmet, clothes and a poncho and a cardboard sign made from a C-ration box. The macabre scarecrow stood along Route 9 for months, symbolizing the savagery of combat. A single lone tall tree standing on the northwest side of the bridge identified the site. Weeks later, the hundreds of NVA dead were buried in two mass graves on the west side of the stream north of Route 9. A few days later the NVA would attack the Cam Lo Combat Base. Again the Duster reactionary force would come to the aid of the Marines at Cam Lo. The battles at base camps across the DMZ and convoy ambushes along Route 9 never stopped in 1968, the "TET YEAR".

January 24, 1968, Dusters shooting at the NVA from Camp Carroll.

After shooting 5,000 40mm rounds at the NVA, the Duster is covered by smoke.

The "lone tree" that represented the apex of the January 24, 1968, ambush "Ground Zero."

This is the bridge the Marine M48 tank crossed before they were hit by NVA RPG's. The Duster was hit by the RPG's before it got to this bridge.

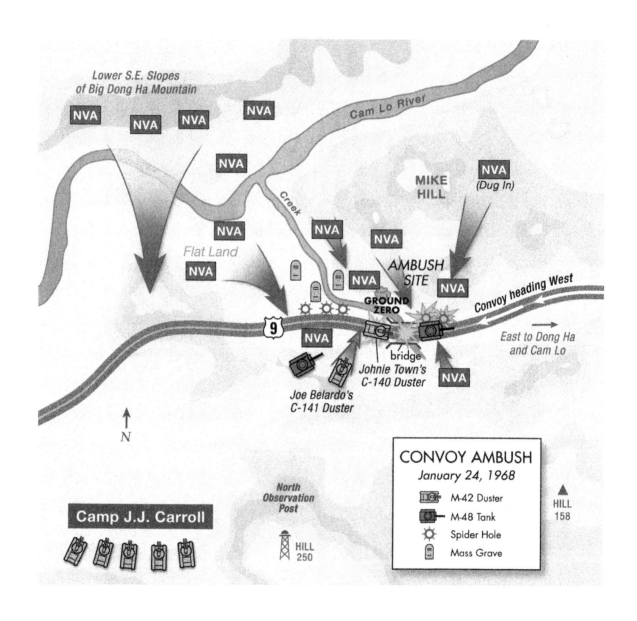

Lower S.E. Slopes
of Big Dong Ha Mountain

Cam Lo River

NVA

NVA   NVA

NVA

NVA

NVA
(Dug In)

Creek

MIKE
HILL

NVA

NVA

NVA

AMBUSH
SITE

Flat Land

NVA

NVA

GROUND
ZERO

NVA

NVA

Convoy heading West

9

NVA

East to Dong Ha
and Cam Lo

bridge
Johnie Town's
C-140 Duster

NVA

Joe Belardo's
C-141 Duster

N

North
Observation
Post

HILL
250

CONVOY AMBUSH

January 24, 1968

M-42 Duster

M-48 Tank

Spider Hole

Mass Grave

HILL
158

Camp J.J. Carroll

NVA soldier being taken out of a spider hole.

Billy Strickland "Killed In Action" – January 24, 1968.

CHAPTER 10: RECOLLECTIONS

I've been trying to sort out the events of the January 24th battle and what went wrong. I was part of a seasoned crew, but the other crew chosen to go down to the ambush had no idea what to expect. Their Squad Leader, Johnny Towns, was the only combat-experienced member on the Duster and was scheduled to go home within the week. This alone was unfair to a short-timer. The Driver, Conley, was not the designated Driver for that track, but only a reactionary force volunteer. He had only been in a few skirmishes and was another short-timer. Lt. Hardin had been advised that our Duster had no starter and had to be towed to start. He knew the shortcomings of Towns' crewmembers and took charge of that Duster himself. He was the Platoon Leader. We had no clear plan and all the cards were stacked up against us. Everyone knew that the ambush was big and bad by the amount of firepower the NVA had already expended trying to destroy the convoy. We also knew it was a bad scene by the thousands and thousands of 40mm shells we had already counter fired at the NVA from Camp Carroll. Both Dusters had already fired thousands of rounds at the ambush site from Camp Carroll and should have been quickly cleaned and re-oiled before leaving camp. The 40mm shells were already jamming in the breaches up at Carroll due to overheating. Lt. Hardin said this was not the time to get squeamish and to *"SADDLE-UP"*.

We all proceeded out the gate of Carroll in high gear. When we were about hundred yards from the ambush, we all came to a stop. We just sat there as ordered, looking and listening. The only shooting was the 40s flying over our heads from Carroll, exploding at some unseen targets to our left. I could feel my jaw muscles tighten and taste my own bile. We were sitting ducks for the NVA.

The Marine Lieutenant and our Lieutenant called all the shots. Sergeant Chester Sines, our Section Chief and the extra man on the crew, repeatedly advised both officers about proper ambush deployment. I begged Towns and Conley not to move and start shooting. The two officers issued orders that they were moving forward and would not chance shooting any Marines who might have taken cover in the brush. Nothing was moving or shooting from the ambushed convoy or from the NVA. It should have been obvious by how quick the enemy knocked out the convoy, that they had a lot of firepower and did not have time to leave the area. They ordered us to hold our positions and await instructions. It was standard combat operating procedure, when in doubt, to shoot the 40s a few hundred yards out past the ambush site and shake up the enemy and see if you got their attention with some return fire. We would put them on the defensive and then assess the situation before committing and moving. Shoot, move, and communicate was our motto. This ambush was too big to be so quiet, and I was very concerned. Sines radioed the lieutenants and suggested we take up position on a small knoll on the south side of the road overlooking the ambush site. It had a small path leading up and down and was wide enough for our track vehicles. This position would give us an advantage if something should happen and still let us be close enough to retrieve the wounded and dead. They were the officers in charge and Chester's suggestions were ignored.

The last radio communication I got from Towns was, "Joe, you guys better cover my ass. I'm short." Towns was referring to his week or so left in country. Screaming into my radio headset, I begged the guys not to advance forward. "Johnny Towns, Billy Conley, what are you fucking crazy? They've never done this before; stay the fuck where you are and start shooting; you know better; we've done this a hundred times together; open up full auto and clear a path and then pick your targets; we will follow your lead and cross over your shells making a big fucking X; you know the drill." The only response we got was from the two lieutenants screaming the words "Move Out". It was the last communication we would ever get.

It was not Americans but NVA who were hidden in the brush. They let the lead M48 tank cross over the small bridge that went over the creek and then blasted it at point blank range with a volley of RPGs (Rocket Propelled Grenades). Before Hardin's Duster could react, the next RPG team blasted them. It was over in less than a minute…the tank and Duster never got a chance to shoot. The NVA were so brazen, they just stood in full view and fired repeatedly. We looked on in horror. We immediately started killing the enemy we could see. In seconds, it became another full size ambush directed at us. RPGs and automatic weapons were now firing at us from everywhere. NVA, swinging satchel charges, sprinted down the road in our direction. Chester and I dropped them with a quick burst of my M-16. Sines screamed at me to get us up on the knoll "NOW!"

The top of the knoll gave us a clear view of the battle area and the elevated firing advantage we needed. Large groups of NVA were running in all directions. As we fought off their attack, Sines was trying to see what needed to be done to retrieve the men from the ambushed convoy. All we needed was some immediate fire support and infantry.

The NVA should not have been allowed to dig in and take ground. We desperately needed additional firepower and ammunition. Sam Lewis handed me his little green book of secret codes from around his neck. As I adjusted the radio frequencies, Chester Sines made the first calls for choppers and air support. As our Duster shot the first obvious enemy targets, Chester and I quickly made circles on my map of the grid coordinates of all the NVA positions we could see. Chester then climbed up the back of the Duster and stood behind the turret pointing at the NVA positions he could see and screaming verbal commands where the Duster should shoot. I radioed Lt. Moore up on Carroll and gave him the grid locations of the enemy. Moore instructed me to radio the four Dusters, who were shooting blindly over our heads from Carroll, and give them targets. Their lines of fire now adjusted, they could sweep the NVA positions effectively. We then gave the same coordinates to the 105mm and 155mm artillery Fire Direction Control at Carroll. All Hell was breaking loose. Our artillery shells, which now began to exploding everywhere, just made the enemy run toward us even faster. They knew, if they got close to us, our large artillery from Carroll could not shoot without killing us. We were going to die. Our orders from Captain Easter at Carroll were vague and non-committal. Our crew could not understand "C" Battery's thinking, and that no other Dusters were immediately sent to help.

We became infuriated with Easter. It was a hard pill to swallow, knowing and feeling you were left to die. Our crew all agreed that we were not going to leave the ambush site without saving the other Duster crew. We thought, if we could fight long enough, Captain Easter would have to send help or body bags. But we were not prepared for the number of NVA we had to fight. The gooks seemed to be coming out of the cracks in the earth. I am amazed at how easy it was shooting them. It was a slaughter, but they did not give an inch. In all the other firefights I had been in, the NVA would try to hide and shoot, hit and run, killing and wounding as many of us as they could and then disappear back into the jungle taking their dead with them. This fight was completely different. They were well equipped with lots of firepower and were here to stay and fight to the end. All of us knew they were headed for Camp Carroll and we had to stop them. If Camp Carroll fell to the enemy, it would be the end of the war.

Even though we were furious at Captain Easter, we all knew, as seasoned combatants, that Easter could not and would not leave Camp Carroll undefended. He had to do what was best, and possibly sacrifice a few men. *Us! So, we were pissed off to say the least.*

We knew we were in deep shit when the NVA bugles and whistles started blowing. Any weapon we fired was effective in killing or wounding the enemy. There were so many NVA that firing one to three 40mm rounds would injure and or kill many enemy soldiers. We would no sooner shoot at one group and another group popped up. As we went from group to group, the first groups we shot could be seen dragging their wounded into the cover of nearby brush or dragging them by a short piece of rope tied to their leg. By the time we traversed back, most of the bodies had disappeared from sight. The NVA did not stop coming and we did not stop killing them. If any got below the line of sight of the 40s, I would shoot them with my M-16 or .45 pistol, or Earl and Dave shot them with the M60 machine gun. The crew was in disbelief when Easter repeated he was not sending help or ammo. Camp Carroll had to be held at all cost. Chester got on the radio and was screaming at him. His screams went unanswered. We had killed or wounded the entire first wave of NVA we could see on each side of the ambushed convoy. As the Duster shot, I just kept doing my job: drive, send radio communications, give firing grids to the artillery, direct the jets and choppers, and shoot my M-16 at any NVA who were getting close to our Duster. It was very eerie how cold and methodical we had become. There were times when we just stopped and waited and nobody was shooting.

Chester or I constantly had to get on the radio and tell the "Bird-Dog" spotter plane that was flying over the area to "go away." We knew he was just trying to help us, but his plane was in the way of the 40s and our artillery shooting at the enemy from Carroll. We were afraid he would be blown out of the sky by one of our shells. Plus, he was in the way of the jet bombing and napalm runs we were trying coordinate. We were glad when he finally left.

There were dead NVA everywhere. It looked like over five hundred, just in the area north of the convoy. Even though the artillery, jets and choppers helped kill the enemy, it felt like just us six and a handful of Marines did most of the killing. I thought we were winning because they had stopped removing their dead from the battlefield. Earl Holt counted 49 dead NVA next to our Duster on the knoll alone. I never counted, but I know only dead NVA were left on that hill. Bodies and parts were strewn everywhere. There would be a pause for a few minutes and then they would start coming again and we would start shooting. With each pause they would rush a little slower, disappearing behind every piece of brush, bush or crevice. It was the most I ever shot my M-16 and .45 pistols. It was the first time I had emptied all my ammo bandoleers of M-16 ammo and had to reload.

To avoid being hit by NVA artillery, we did a sporadic stop-and-go all over the knoll. It was impossible, as we dodged artillery, not to run over some of the NVA bodies. On the east side of the creek, we could see a small group of NVA advancing toward the convoy. We shot at them with our M60 but could not shoot the 40s because the shrapnel from them would hit the convoy. Out of nowhere, a small group of villagers and Montagnard people started running across the battlefield, heading for their homes at Cam Lo. It was amazing, everyone stopped shooting. It caused a semi-pause in the battle. We screamed and yelled for them to run as fast as they could and get out of the way. Everyone seemed to be regrouping. We were almost out of ammo and still hoped for relief. Because we could not shoot, the NVA began feverishly picking up their dead and wounded, and disappeared with them back into the brush. They had to know we were low on ammo, but they did not risk the test under fire. Our 40mm ack-ack guns had ripped them virtually to pieces. We now just stared at each other and waited. As the NVA ran out from their cover, we shot them with our M-16s. If we had been given the ammo we requested, this would have been the only time we could have evacuated the men trapped in the ambush. As history was being written, the wait for ammo was too long and neither side was retreating.

When Easter finally allowed the first group of volunteers to try and bring us ammo, it was too late. The NVA could be seen regrouping and were advancing very slowly. We had stopped shooting the 40mm, because we were down to only a few clips of 40 ammo. We shot our M-16 and took turns shooting the M60 machine gun. It was an awful feeling, this waiting to die. I began to wonder how I would die and what gook was finally going to kill me. I kept telling myself ***"I'm not going to let them take me alive."*** Our situation was not very good. The phrase ***"Wha'd'ya think?"*** must have been said a thousand times. Nobody really gave a shit what we thought. I thought we were just NVA bait. We were going to finally be overrun, and die. ***"Wha'd'ya think?"***

Lt. Steve Moore was now up on OP Hill 250 with Lou Block's Duster crew. Hill 250 overlooked the ambush site and had the best field of view. Chester and I again coordinated with Moore the counter battery fire against the enemy. Moore knew what to do and would give us all the protection he could. There was only one problem. They could visually see us but could not lower the guns enough to clear the enemy that surrounded our Duster and the convoy area. Like the other

Dusters at Carroll, they could only shoot and cover an area about three-hundred yards from us and out to the Cam Lo River and slopes of Dong Ha mountain. Our crew agreed that we could not let our friends, who were coming to help us, drive the ammo truck into the main ambush area below our knoll and be killed. Plus, we could not risk driving our Duster back down onto Route 9 because we now had no more 40 ammo and could not take or fight back another direct NVA assault. The ammo truck driver, Bob "Willy" Williams, and Don Wolfe, riding shotgun with an M-60, didn't know exactly where we were. One of us had to try to get to them before they drove directly into the ambush site and were killed.

I am not sure how I was selected to run down the hill to Route 9 and *"fetch"* the first ammo truck. Some say I volunteered. My crew said they just pointed at me and off I went. I'm not really sure, and it really does not matter. I filled my pockets with grenades, wrapped two bandoleers of M-16 ammo around me, and attached my bayonet before descending down the hill. I thought if I went on an angle, away from the ambush site and yet towards the road, I would go somewhat unnoticed by the NVA and stop the truck before it got too close. As I ran down the hill, my pants were falling off from the weight of the grenades. I guess I was a little overloaded and had to hold my pants up with one hand and hold my M-16 with the other hand. I used all the little things they teach you in boot camp: running in a zigzag, low crawling, rolling, and counting before you throw the grenades, shooting single shots and short bursts, and bayonet training.

I finally had to stop and pull up my pants. I had just killed a handful of gooks and needed to regroup and get my bearings and fix my pants. Lying on my back against a small dirt hill, I pulled up my pants and tightened the belt. I now could hear Vietnamese language, and what I thought was French, being spoken on the other side of the hill I had to go down. Trying to stay unnoticed, I shimmied up under some brush. Straining to get a better look, I could only see legs, boots and a very tall guy in a beige uniform talking and pointing up the hill. I pulled the pin of one grenade and tossed it over the hill. I closely watched the grenade as it slowly sailed through the air and prayed I had given it a good enough toss and that it wouldn't come back down on top of me. I quickly followed with two more tosses. After the explosions, I quickly crawled up over the hill. A small group of NVA lay dead and wounded in the small depression. Without counting them or searching them, I quickly shot them again and continued my run down the hill to Route 9. Things were so crazy and confusing going down that hill. I could hear NVA yelling and screaming, their whistles and bugles blowing. I would run a few yards and hide behind some cover before advancing again. My heart was pounding out of my chest as the NVA walked past without noticing me. I shot the little bastards in the back. It was too late to change my mind or direction. I was now about a hundred yards from my Duster. I just shot at anything that moved or I thought was moving. To this day, I don't think they were prepared for one Army idiot assaulting them. They were caught completely off guard. Plus, I could run real fast, as it was all downhill. Maybe that helped.

When I got to Route 9, I took cover in the drainage ditch on the south side of the road. I wasn't sure what to do and was exhausted. My mind told me not to make any noise and take time to regroup. This was the first time I was truly ever alone in Vietnam, and the first time I had done anything like this. I was not in the infantry. All kinds of crazy thoughts ran through my mind. Should I advance west towards the approaching ammo truck or wait for it to arrive? I didn't know what to do. How many more gooks could I kill before they killed me? I had a good view up Route 9 and was concealed from view, so I decided to wait, and when I saw the truck coming, I would wave it down.

Within minutes, I saw six NVA soldiers on the other side of the road walking slowly in a crouched position towards my direction. My heart was pounding out of my chest. They had no idea that I was sitting less than a 100 feet from them. Occasionally, they stopped and ducked their heads like turtles and crouched as Moore's 40s from Hill 250 and Camp Carroll hit the areas behind them. They just pointed up at Camp Carroll and again started moving forward slowly, using hand signals. They had grass sticking out of their helmets and waistbands, with bandoleers around their chests. I held my breath and took aim at the gook in the middle of the group. As the next volley of artillery exploded, I shot. They quickly ducked. I think they thought they were shot at from our group on the knoll or hit by the shrapnel from the exploding artillery. They had no idea how their friend got killed and they seemed not to care. I was amazed that they never ran to or even gave any real aid to their fallen comrade. They were hard Sons-of-Bitches. They never made the next 50 feet or knew who shot them. Remaining in the ditch for what seemed to be an eternity, I prayed that my friends would find my remains if I got killed. Hearing a lot of shooting and explosions from the direction of the ammo truck, I ran down the road a few 100 feet and took cover again in the ditch. I could see the ammo truck being riddled by NVA heavy weapons fire. As Don Wolfe blasted away with his M60, killing the NVA rushing the truck, another group of NVA charged the truck from both sides, wounding Don and a few other guys. All I could do was pick off a few NVA with my M-16 as I looked on in horror, crying and watching from my hiding position, as my friends got hurt and maybe killed trying to help me. Unable to fight their way past the NVA, the truck was forced to turn around and limp back to Carroll. ***I felt totally helpless and ashamed that I could not help them.*** I quickly started back up the hill.

My memory has always been good, but maybe a portion of my brain got fried on the way down or toasted when I climbed out of the ditch along the road and started back up the hill. All I remember are the screams and that horrible silence when their screaming stopped. The only sound I remember hearing was my heart pounding. Everything around me went into slow motion. A feeling of unbelievable loneliness and hopelessness overwhelmed me. Then I finally went into the, "I don't give a shit, I'm dead." mode. We all want to survive and I was in survival mode. Lots of NVA died on my runs down and up that horrible hill, more than I care to remember or want to write in my diary. I made friends and blood brothers with the Devil today and can only hope that God forgives me. As they say, my name wasn't at the top of His list. I hope my Mom forgives me if she ever reads this diary.

I was bloody from what I thought were cuts and scrapes from running through the brush and crawling past the dead NVA. It was more frightening to run back up the hill. The Marines were shooting at anything or anybody coming up that hill. Constantly, I yelled my name, "New Jersey," and any other American name I could think of. As I ran and crawled back up the hill, I rested and took cover next to the dead NVA, using their bodies as a shield and protection from both the NVA and Marine bullets. I could feel the bullets hitting the bodies and feared they would come through and kill me. If I thought they were still alive, I would shoot the NVA again before advancing. It was hard getting back up the hill.

When I was finally close enough for the Marines and my Duster brothers to get a good look at me, I stood all the way up in the **"I surrender"** position, with my rifle over my head. I walked slowly up the center of the path, screaming my name and silently praying on the inside not to be killed by my fellow Americans or the NVA. I never held my breath so long. My comrades finally motioned to me and waved me up the hill. I ran like Hell. I told my crew what had happened, swapped positions with Sines, and started driving again around the knoll. I then called Camp Carroll to find out *WHAT THE HELL HAPPENED?*

The Marines, who were with us, wanted to withdraw up the hill, straight to Outpost Hill 250 or Camp Carroll. NVA artillery, RPGs, and recoilless cannon shells were now landing everywhere. Sines convinced them to hold on a little longer. The waiting seemed endless. The radio crackled full of chatter. Duster crews from the Khe Gio Bridge, Rockpile and Ca Lu were calling and volunteering to help their friends. It was pure chaos and had become out of control. Radio language was now on a first-name basis.

Our Battalion Commander, Lieutenant Colonel John House, ordered all radio frequencies cleared and exclusively used for battle communications. Thank God, House's courageous orders brought the battle back to military standards. He was sending reactionary reinforcements from Dong Ha, under the guidance of Captain Easter at Carroll. We thought that LTC House's brave combat decision was going to save everyone in the kill zone. I gave credit to the Colonel, for a decision that could possibly have saved hundreds of Americans and Camp Carroll.

The Marine from The Water Point, Roger Blentlinger, radioed our Duster to say that another volunteer Reactionary Group was coming from Carroll. I radioed back and gave him a different radio frequency to use. We all knew each other and did not need or want to use proper military radio language. The radio barked: "Joe, this is Roger. Tank and I are coming down with some volunteers, two truckloads of ammo, a squad of Marines, and Medic "Doc" Butler. We're not exactly sure where you are or what your situation is, but we're coming down. Hold tight, buddy, and give us a sign where you guys are." I radioed back and spoke with Tank and told him where I would meet them on the road. He was a fellow Road Warrior and knew the location.

The NVA had now moved really close to the knoll. Because we had no 40mm ammo, we could not stop them. We were saving the balance of our personal ammo for a face-to-face confrontation. We did not want this ammo truck and volunteer rescue team to run into the advancing NVA. One more time, I ran down that Godforsaken hill to Route 9. This time I took one of the small paths back to the road. I was running so fast that my forward momentum was causing me to stumble. As I ran and stumbled down the hill, an NVA soldier out of nowhere attacked me from my back right side. As he jumped on me, he tried to stab me with his knife and ended up hitting my M-16. His next swing cut my left wrist. I quickly let go of my rifle and grabbed his arm. Scared shitless, we went falling and rolling, head over heels, down the hill. I never let go of his arm or the hand holding the knife. Kicking and screaming, we both fought for our lives. I quickly sent him to his maker. Struggling to get back up on my feet, another gook poked at me with his screwdriver pointed bayonet pig sticker and hit me in the right forearm. Kicking him in his knee, he fell backwards. Scrambling for my life, I finally got off a shot with my .45 and sent him flying on his ass. Crawling on my belly, I recovered my M-16 and shot him again as he tried to get back up. Frightened out of my mind and trying to catch my breath and get my bearings, I got back on my feet and I ran over to the first guy and shot him in the head. The two NVA were either out of ammo or trying to take me prisoner, God only knows. Running like a crazy man, who just escaped from a mental hospital, I continued down the path.

After what seemed like another eternity of shooting, running, ducking, crawling and cursing, I reached the road. In my haste to get away from the enemy, I was nowhere near my original goal on the road. Instead, I was on a ledge about six feet high overlooking my destination. Running full speed downhill, I had no choice and leaped off the ledge like a flying squirrel sailing through the air. I landed on my ass in front of the approaching ammo truck, only to be shot at by Roger. *Thank God he missed.* Tank stopped the truck just short of running me over. I directed them back to the top of the knoll, taking the same path back I took on my first run. Getting the ammo truck up the hill was another nightmare. I could not believe the fuckin' truck got stuck in a small ditch. *I just couldn't believe it.* I told Tank to take over and get the Marines in a fighting position. I'd be back with the Duster. *It was a living nightmare.* Cursing and screaming, I sprinted back up the hill. This time I just ran until I got back to my Duster. After all, it made no difference; we were all dead men walking. If my friends or the Marines shot me, no one gave a shit at this point. Friendly fire or enemy, it made no difference now how I died.

My Duster crew could not believe what had just happened and headed down the hill to the trucks, the M-60 blazing a trail. As we hooked up our tow cable to the truck, Chester quickly explained to the Marine Lt. what the situation was and what needed to be done.

Finally back on top of the knoll, with our new supply of ammo and reinforcements, we started to shoot back at the advancing NVA. As we shot, the reinforcement crew refilled the Duster with 40mm ammo. They could not believe how many NVA we had killed. Bodies and body parts were growing everywhere. Everyone was screaming and yelling and cursing and crying. In true Duster Gunfighter Tradition, our crew stood brazenly, defying the NVA to kill us, as we humped ammo and fired our guns at the advancing enemy. Enemy bugles and whistles blowing added an eerie soundtrack to the killing of other humans, as NVA bodies were mutilated by our high explosive 40mm shells.

My brain still screams when I think of that horrible day. I still hear the clacking of rifle butts against rifle butts, and butts against flesh, as we dueled for our lives. We just stood there doing our jobs as the enemy bombs exploded around us and endless bullets pinged off the Duster. We all knew this could be our last day on earth as each man made constant eye contact and stood tall to his task of killing. Chester, now on the radio, was informed that a relief force from Dong Ha was being sent to rescue the destroyed convoy, the Marine tank, and Lt. Hardin's Duster with Johnny Towns' crew. But, they never mentioned us. Chester looked at me and said, "I don't think the reactionary force even knows where we are, or even that we are here at all." I got on the radio and asked for another sit-rep and got the same answer. I then called again and tried to get the radio frequency of the approaching reactionary team and their call sign. The radio operator advised us that the Captain Easter's orders were not to communicate with us, because he did not want to compromise the mission. We couldn't believe what we just heard. It didn't matter. We would be dead by the time they got here. All we wanted to do was tell the reactionary force not to charge into the ambush site and where the enemy was now situated. We were never given the opportunity and knew in our hearts that another Duster crew was being sent to their death.

Since this could be our last hurrah, I climbed into the turret behind Sam Lewis and started to load the 40. The guns were really hot and the 40s were self-detonating as they entered the firing chamber. Constantly, Earl Holt and I took turns reaching into the red hot breaches and un-jamming the stuck 40 rounds, the hot shells and loading chambers burning our fingers and arms. Earl said he thought we might have some oil in the outside storage compartment or on the trucks. Giving his loading task to David Lewis, he went for the oil. We continued to pick off enemy 57 recoilless cannons and RPG teams, their shells flying over our heads like giant smoking bottle rockets. Sam Lewis yelled, "Duck," as he saw another NVA shoot his 57 recoilless directly at us. The enemy shell hit the ground next to our Duster. The exploding shell hit us with hot shrapnel and debris. I thought the skin was burned off my body by the explosion. I stood there frantically patting my chest, arms and face. There were at least three or four more explosions. I remember being thrown on top of the 40mm breach and trying to sit up. Then there was another horrific noise as both our cannons exploded. It was a mess.

I now found myself on top of Sam with a long thin toothpick piece of metal from my own guns sticking out of the right cheek of my ass. It was hard to regroup. My ears were ringing and I was dizzy from the explosion. I was trying so hard to remember where I was and what had just happened. In a blurry daze, I pulled out the piece of shrapnel in my ass. Standing, I felt something hit me in my left underarm, twisting me in a bent position over the edge of the turret. Struggling to stand, I looked around. At first I saw no one and thought the explosions had killed the rest of the crew. Then I noticed David standing there covered in blood with a long piece of shrapnel sticking through the bridge of his nose. He slowly fell backwards between the Duster and the ammo truck. I thought he was dead. No one else was in sight. They had been blown off the Duster and ammo truck. I was still trying to regroup and orientate myself and was really groggy and fucked up. It felt like all my corpuscles were exploding inside me. Everything was going in slow motion. As I bent over, trying to keep from fainting, I noticed Sam slumped over the Gunner's turret crank. Our helmets had been blown off by the explosions. The skin on the side of Sam's head had been peeled to the back of his head. I thought he was dead. Blood was everywhere and all you could hear was screaming and yelling and the faint distant sound of more NVA whistles and bugles. Hot shrapnel peppered us as the NVA shells continued to explode all around us.

I soon realized that the blood dripping on Sam's head was mine. I now thought the enemy had blown out my brains and shot me full of holes, and that I had lost my right eye. Smoke seemed to be coming out of me and my flak jacket. I started patting myself again like a madman, trying to put out the unseen fire. Frantically, I pulled the long slivers of shrapnel out of my head, the corner of my eye, my nose, and mouth. I then started choking on my own blood. When I felt my face, I thought the hole by my right eyebrow went into my brain. I started screaming and cursing at the fucking gook bastards for blowing my brains out. The turret was swinging wildly and I thought it was on fire, so I pulled the turret fire extinguishers. Yanking Sam out of the Gunner's seat, I jumped off the Duster and ran with Sam slumped over my shoulder, as I shot at the NVA. A Marine helped us and dragged us away from enemy fire to the back of the trucks. Doc Butler quickly revived Sam with mouth to mouth, and the Marine helped him apply bandages to my head, arms and chest. For some reason, I got back in the turret and grabbed the M60 machine gun off the turret mount and started shooting at the NVA. I really was just trying to stay alive.

Earl, John, and Roger joined me in the turret with their M-16. Things were happening faster than most of the guys could react. I think we were all in total survival mode and running on energy from the final fear of dying. We all now fought like wild savages, each of us screaming, howling, laughing and cursing as we fed off each other's courage. As we killed the enemy, Chester Sines ordered the others to collect our dead and wounded and put them in or on the trucks, tank and Duster. ***Sines screamed, "Prepare to fight your way through the advancing NVA; we're going back to Carroll or die."*** Sines radioed Carroll advising them we were hit, out of commission, and were coming back. We had not recovered the other Duster and M48 Tank. To this day, we don't know how we did it. We had cut a path through the advancing NVA and back to Camp Carroll. It was something we all will never forget. Like true Grim Reapers, we harvested the enemy.

When we finally got back to Carroll, the first thing we did was insist that Sam and David get immediate medical help. We then tried to get more Dusters and Quad-50 machine guns to go back down to the ambush and retrieve our friends. We ran around, crazed with the lust to fight and to kill more enemy and save our friends. Sines advised us that we were ordered to stop and stand-down. The reactionary force from

Dong Ha had arrived at the ambush site. **We** all went crazy, screaming and yelling how we wanted to be the ones who saved our men, our friends. The rescuers should have been from Charlie Battery, not some reactionary force guys from Dong Ha. **We** had fought so hard. **We** had killed so many. **We** had shed our blood. They kept insisting I get medivaced, and we insisted on seeing Captain Easter. Finally exhausted, I sat on the sandbag wall by Paul "Boston" Conley's tent and bummed a cigarette and some water. Paul just stared at me and patted my back. I was not trying to be a martyr or a hero. I knew I was wounded, but not bad, and just looked like shit. Doc Butler was now covering my forehead, right eye, and forearms with field dressings and telling me he wanted me medivaced. A bandage was wrapped tight at my left armpit where I was shot by a ricochet or a small piece of shrapnel. One tooth was broken off and a little blood was coming out of my ears, eyes and broken nose. The back of my flak jacket was hanging off, and my clothes looked like shredded wheat covered in blood. My butt felt like a pincushion from my own Duster blowing up and peppering my ass - "the final insult".

I was very lucky that my wounds were not life threatening. I looked a lot worse then I felt, but really was in shock and running on adrenaline. Being covered in an extra layer of dirt and black ash, from the exploding NVA shells and our own 40mm rounds exploding, made me look like someone who just walked out of Hell.

Captain Easter finally met us outside the Command Bunker. He just stood there, staring at us in disbelief. We must have been some sight. I will never forgive him for telling us how to report what we did and saw. He instructed us not to upset everyone and to say very little. He ordered us to say that we had encountered a small group of NVA, and that our guns had jammed and blown up before we could rescue the other Duster.

For some stupid reason, or maybe because of all the confusion, we let him have his way. *He was the Captain*. The jamming and blowing up of our guns would be our only recognition. We were then accused of abandoning our comrades and running back to camp during a firefight. In the bunker, he interrogated us as if we had done something wrong.

Everybody in the Command Bunker was shooting questions so fast that we could not reply in time. ***My heart was broken***. We sat with our heads bowed in disbelief, giving the tribunal one-word answers we thought Easter wanted us to say. I wanted to explode and beat the shit out of all those guys. I thought they were supposed to be our friends. ***Who the hell did they think they were?*** They had no clue what we had done, what had happened, or what was happening down at the ambush. They were twisting the truth to save their own chicken-shit butts and poor combat decisions. It was now late, so I finally asked to be transported to the medivac station. A chopper took me to Dong Ha.

After arriving at "D" Med in Dong Ha, I could not find my wounded crewmembers and asked one of the Corpsman what happened to the first wave of wounded. He told me they had already been shipped out, either to one of the hospital ships, the Repose or the Sanctuary, or to the hospitals in DaNang. I saw the crew from Johnny Towns' Duster. It was hectic and noisy, doctors screaming orders trying to save lives. Johnny just stood there with powder burns down his side. He looked like a burnt marshmallow. He was trying to get the best aid he could for his injured crew. I assured him that everything was going to be okay. We hugged and he thanked me for saving them. He told me we were the ones who kept the NVA off them. Johnny was a great soldier and a natural leader. He stayed with his men to the end. Wounded and dead soldiers from the reactionary force lay next to Gilbert, who had lost his arms, and Solomon, who had big holes through his legs. Vince DeSantis, a former "C" Battery person, had upper body wounds and didn't look too good. I gave each of them a few words of encouragement and a hug. A few others I did not know were waiting for treatment. I was deeply saddened when I learned that Billy Strickland was killed. DeSantis said that an RPG had smoked their Driver, Carr. I looked around, but could not find him. I then went over to Graves Registration and said a prayer over my dead friends. Standing outside and alone, crying, I was enraged to see all of my friends lying there wounded, mutilated or dead. This would not have happened if Command had listened to us Road Warriors. After a while I was treated and sent to Da Nang and spent a few days in the hospital getting some needed body repairs before being allowed to return to Camp Carroll. I never again saw the wounded guys from Johnny Towns' crew or Tedesco's reactionary crew.

January 24, 1968 was an unforgettable day. I have dreamed a million times about this battle. It seemed that there was no other battle in Duster history that surpassed this tragic day. Yet, it was just another day for the Duster Road Warriors. At all the reunions, this battle is rekindled and the Dragon of War is allowed to breathe flames once more. In the eyes of our crew, someone just waited a little too long to make a commitment to action. The hierarchy seemed to shudder at the mere thought of either screwing up, having death on their hands, or losing more of Uncle Sam's equipment. War is not fair or just and has no conclusion but victory or defeat. Some soldiers never engaged the enemy up close and are curious and eager for the gory details of battle. They don't know how lucky they are. I push right past that memory and on to the rest of the saga. I tell myself, it was just another day in "The Nam". I guess it was so terrifying that my mind protects me from the memory - most of the time. I didn't think I had recovered from the January 13th battle and probably will never fully recover from the January 24th battle.

The smell of the dead NVA still lingers in my nose. How odd.

Twenty years later, in 1988, I finally received the actual Purple Heart medal. I was thankful that the Marines had sent my father a letter attesting to my wounds and informing him that I had received a Purple Heart. It was instrumental in my finally getting the Purple Heart Medal.

In 1998, I saw Johnny Towns for the first time since the war. We hugged and cried and jumped around like two little kids. It was an unbelievably great feeling. I met his wife and other members of his family. His family was curious about Johnny's wild tales of the war. John (Tank) Huelsenbeck and I told them about all the different war experiences the three of us had together. What was once an unreal war story now gave him credibility. Johnny's family beamed with joy, admiration and love. After waiting 35 years to be decorated, Towns was finally awarded his Purple Heart and Bronze Star in November 2003 with the help of Lt. Steve Moore.

CHAPTER 11: G.I. JOE ROLLS ON

February 1: Robert "Billy" Conley was killed today. I became hysterical when I got the call on our radio. I had promised Conley that, on his last day in the combat zone, I would lead his convoy to the safety of Dong Ha and get him home safe and in one piece. His memory haunts me. I wasn't there to lead him home. He was killed halfway to Dong Ha. I blame myself for his death.

Norman Oss, another Duster Driver, and I still cry when we think of him.

I was told Lt. Steve Moore went home, only to be reassigned as one of the officers who knocked on the door to tell the parents that their son died in the war. It was hard enough for him to fight the enemy, get wounded, and lose some of his men, but now this……. Why?!

I guess Uncle Sam thought someone had to do it – why not him?

They told us that Camp J.J. Carroll had been hit by hundreds of NVA artillery shells everyday for the last twenty-eight days. While I was recovering from my wounds, we were given a new Duster called "Float 4." This Duster is completely refurbished and looks brand new. No dents, no holes, engine runs great and there is no play in the turret, making it shoot straight as an arrow. Plus, it is the fastest Duster and can hit 54 mph.

I cannot believe I have survived this long. I've been in so many firefights that I have lost count. One battle just rolls into another. It seems an endless ordeal. How much more do they expect us to handle? How many more do they want us to kill?

Twenty-nine years would pass before a handful of us from Charlie Battery would meet Moore and Amerman in Washington, DC, on Veterans Day at "The Wall." Our meeting was much more than we had anticipated. The hugs and tears allowed our guards to drop for just a moment. It was filled with deep friendship and a personal bond of mutual respect and understanding. Hand on top of hand, we rubbed our fingers over each carved granite name of our departed friends. As we rubbed each name, we said their names aloud, bringing their memory back to life for just a moment as our minds drifted back to slaying Dragons together in a far away land. The magic of "The Black Granite Wall" reached out to us, making all of us even closer to the covenant called "Nam".

February 2: Cam Lo Base Camp was half overrun by the NVA, proof that they had not left the area. A couple of Quads got hit by RPGs. Again, Duster reactionary forces from Dong Ha helped save the day. My good friends, Hollis Hale and Johnnie Sheares from the Quad 50s, were killed in the battle.

February 5: The Rockpile was hit by twenty NVA rockets. Captain Easter accused me of prematurely pulling the fire extinguisher in the turret during the battle. This was the straw that broke my back. Seven months of blood and guts came to a head. How could I be so stupid as to think the Duster was on fire, when it was only the 40s that were blowing up in the turret and burning?! We still had half a tank of gasoline. What did he fucking think, gas wouldn't burn? I went berserk and totally out of control. As he ran into the command bunker, I was screaming how I was going to kick his sorry fucking ass across the DMZ. I now stood in front of the Command Bunker, screaming obscenities. "You can give me all your shit missions, but I am not going to let you accuse me or my crew of any other wrong doings." I bellowed. "You can kiss my Italian ass. Come out of the fuckin' Command Bunker, you chicken-shit-mother-fucker. We did all your fuckin' dirty work. It's time for you to get a little bloody. No guns, no knives, no sticks, and no stones, just simple hand-to-hand, man-to-man, "up front and personal". I'll show you what it's like to get a real ass kicking. I'll give you a beating that you'll remember for the rest of their lives. Then you can give yourself a Purple Heart." All I wanted to do was what I called *"play"* and I am real good at *"playing"*. I am no longer going to allow them to break our spirit or accuse my crew of something we did not do or deserve.

They sent big Dave Woods out to try to calm me down. Dave and I were friends from boot camp. I told poor Dave I was not in the mood. He did not want a piece of me, not today. After a short conversation, I finally walked back to my bunker, mumbling to myself.

February 7: Dusterman Robert Coates was killed. I feel bad that I didn't get a chance to know him better. He was from one of the other firing Batteries.

February 8: Our crew was called to the CP (Command Post) for another debriefing of the January 24th battle. I thought we were in trouble again. An officer I did not know but had seen around camp did all the talking. To our surprise, the officer reported how courageous we had all fought and how proud he was of us and Charlie Battery. The officer went into some detail about the strength of the enemy we had fought and some battle statistics. He further explained how important our role was in this war, and how he was personally going to see that all of us got proper recognition and medals. We had successfully defended the enemy from taking Camp Carroll. The officers talked to Chester and me for a long time and took notes. We each wrote a story about the battle. Our letter was short and brief. It was a good meeting.

***I wrote my Dad another letter marked "Personal".

Dear Dad,
How are you? Fine I hope. I am also fine. I know you are probably wondering how I got wounded again. This isn't the first time things like this happen around here and won't be the last. Well, here goes. January 24th, the convoy got hit going from Dong Ha to Camp Carroll. It was almost here when it got hit. Our track and another were called to go help pull them out. To make a very long story short, we drove up almost to the ambush site. The other track and a tank with us went right into the ambush. Before we knew it, that tank and track got hit with RPGs (they blow tanks apart). It was real bad. Dad, we tried to get them out. The fighting was furious. We were outnumbered and just couldn't get to them. We pulled on top of this small hill overlooking

the ambush. They started hitting us with everything they had: rifles, RPGs, mortars and recoilless rifle cannons. We never stopped trying to save our friends. We finally got hit by a couple of their cannons. That's what wounded most of us. The blast also caused both our twin 40mm cannons to explode, making us useless. Dad, we kept fighting with our rifles and hands, it was tough going. We had to fight our way back to our camp. I wish you could meet my friends. You would really like them. They're a great bunch of very brave guys. As they say, "That's all she wrote." At our last briefing, we were told that, at the end of the battle, there were four hundred of the enemy killed. Half of the Marine unit we were trying to help were wounded or wiped out. Three tracks, a tank, and many trucks were destroyed, and some Army personnel (us) were killed and wounded. Since then, we're running the roads even more, becoming regular roadrunners. We get hit every day at Camp Carroll. Well, that's about all, Dad. Don't worry; I know the ropes of the game. Since I have been here, life has a new look for me. I'm a real lucky guy to have parents like you and Mom. The saying that fits this place goes like this, "To really live, you must nearly die". Thanks, Dad, for everything you've done for me.

Love you,

Your son

xxxxx

February 9: We were one of two Dusters assigned as the security team to guard the Marine engineers who were being sent down to the January 24th ambush site to clean up the dead NVA. As we stood guard, a bulldozer dug two long trenches like a letter "L" on the north side of Route 9. One was parallel to Route 9 just west of the lone tree we called ground zero during the ambush. The other was dug parallel to the small creek north of the lone tree. It was a horrible sight watching the Marines collect the NVA bodies and throw them in the trenches. The smell was disgusting. They dragged one of the NVA out of the ditch that ran along the road and tied him to the concrete road marker that was engraved with the words Dong Ha and an arrow pointing east. I wondered if it was one of the gooks I had shot. They dressed him in a fatigue shirt and pants, a helmet, and a pair of Tank Driver's goggles. They put a cigarette in his mouth and placed a sign dangling from his neck that read "Fuck with the Marines – Die like the Rest".

One of the Marine units guarded the area for a few months. As the NVA body decomposed, passing convoys would stop and rebuild the "Road Marker of War," keeping the symbol of the carnage from the 24th alive, by using empty brass cannon shells as legs and Vietnamese grass knives as arms.

February 10: An NVA artillery shell exploded next to Earl. Earl went flying and flipping through the air about thirty feet. He was lying there motionless on his left side, knocked unconscious from the blast with a big piece of shrapnel protruding through his flak jacket into his heart. Thinking he was dead, we slowly rolled him onto his back to see if there was anything we could do to save him. After a close examination, and to our total amazement, the shrapnel was stuck through his flak jacket and into his pocket Bible he carried in his fatigue pocket over his heart. He had just been knocked out and was badly bruised. We all stood there in disbelief looking at each other. It took a few minutes before he woke up and regrouped his senses. He never knew what hit him, so we had to explain over and over what had happened, until it finally registered in his rattled brain. We never heard the end of it. God's Bible had saved his life and now we had to pray even more with him. We appeased him by telling him to have his Mom send us a case of Bibles. I am glad Earl survived. We have become great friends. I pray I will never see him get killed or severely wounded.

Dear God, please protect my crew and my friends. Never take them to your palace until they are very old men and have lived a full life. When they come to you, please let them sit in Heaven at your right side. They are all good men, God. They have only disobeyed your teachings because it is war and they live here in Hell with me. If you have to blame someone God, blame me. I have taken them down another path and forced them to obey my rules. God, I promise I will do my best to keep them safe and still believe in you and your teachings. God, please keep a place open for me on your left, we need to talk.

February 11: Dusters at Ca Lu destroyed four NVA bunkers.

February 12: On this day, I was training one of the guys named Danny to be a Driver. I went through all the basics with him. Because the Duster has an automatic transmission, it was easy to drive. It had low, high, neutral, reverse, park and a gear that made the Duster turn 360 degrees in a complete circle. It was not hard to get it going and you steered it with a bicycle handlebar. I explained that, to be a good driver, you must think you are slow dancing with a beautiful girl and push the steering bar real slow as though you were sashaying her across the dance floor. Don't jerk it or you will give whiplash to the guys up in the turret. We decided that we would practice combat conditions and requirements another day. He jumped in the Driver's seat and I sat next to him in the TC seat. We drove around Camp Carroll for about a half hour, practicing shifting from low to high and stopping. He seemed to be getting the feel of the Duster but, like all new guys, was still very nervous. He was used to being up in the turret loading the 40s, not driving. We were driving from the southern back area of Carroll up the long straight-a-way road that lead back to the main gate and our position. I told him to ride on the right side of the shallow drainage ditch that ran alongside the road because there was a convoy assembling and lining up to leave Carroll.

We no sooner crossed the ditch when the first volley of NVA artillery shells hit Carroll, exploding to our far right. As usual, they were trying to zero in on the assembling convoy. I told him to speed it up and get back to our position in case there was also a ground attack. For some unexplainable reason, he slammed on the brakes and jumped off the Duster and into the ditch face down, digging for China with his bare hands. I kept screaming at him to get back in the Duster and I would drive. Frozen with fear, he just laid there. Marines, trying to avoid the flying shrapnel, started jumping out of the convoy trucks into the same ditch. Sprinting up and down the length of the ditch, I was screaming at the Marines to get back in their trucks and get the Hell out of Carroll, because the enemy was trying to hit the convoy. I could see the next volley hit closer to our ditch. A few of the Marines got their trucks moving and some still lay in the ditch, hoping the enemy artillery would miss them. The next volley sent me flying in the air and covered me in smoldering dirt and black smoke. Landing with a hard thud and out of breath, I saw another shell land on the Marines in our ditch, about three hundred feet in front of me. Everybody started running for their lives in all different directions, as the NVA walked the shells down the ditch. I grabbed Danny by the scruff of his neck and dragged him screaming with fear through the next volley of artillery explosions. I then threw him head first into the TC hatch of the Duster. In high gear, I drove back to our position through another volley of exploding shells and parked the Duster in its three-sided parapet home.

Now totally pissed off and out of control, I yanked Danny out of the TC hatch, dragged him to our bunker and threw him inside, head-over-heels. Our Section Chief Chester Sines took cover in our bunker. As the bombs continued to explode all around us, I screamed that Chester best get rid of this guy or I would kill him. Ranting and raving, Earl held me back from kicking his ass. Still screaming, I told everybody to get on the Duster and see if they could see where the enemy was shooting from and shoot back and kill the bastards. "Chester, Danny stays in the fuckin' bunker and you do his job or else I'll have to shoot him *and* you." After the smoke cleared, I visited Roger at the Water Point and told him what happened. Roger just smiled and said "Joe, what-da-ya-fuckin'-expect-from-some-fuckin'-doggie-Army guy?" "Roger, I'm in the Army." "See, what did I tell you in the past – you guys are all fucked up." I just laughed and said "gimme some of that good liquid you Marines call drinking water."

February 14: Lou Block's track C121, while shooting at an NVA rocket position, took a direct hit on the rear deck. Four of Block's crew were wounded. It was Lou's lucky day; he didn't get a scratch.

February 17: Our position was hit by seven NVA rockets. I hate those damn things. The men now had a new saying about the enemy "Kill Them All, Let God Sort Them Out".

February 20: Our new Duster, "Float 4", ran over a mine. The NVA tried to finish us off with some close mortar rounds. They blew some holes through the turret, hitting Earl Holt and Dave Lewis with shrapnel. When we finally got back to Carroll, we had to cut off Earl's boot to fix his wounds. He is okay but needs a new pair of boots. Every crewmember now has a "Purple Heart" or three. Dave Lewis' Purple Heart would be his ticket to a Duster unit in the Saigon area. Damn, I am going to miss Float 4.

February 23: Our crew hitched a ride on a convoy to Dong Ha and got another Duster. At Dong Ha, I inquired about my personnel records and was informed they were not to be found and must have been destroyed **again.** Those records would be the only evidence of my service to my country. My father always showed me his from WW-II. I wanted to share the same experience with him and my future children. Plus, I wanted the Army to confirm the day I was supposed to go home. I guessed they'll keep me here until I die.

February 25: I was called to attend an awards formation. Captain Tedesco pinned on our Purple Hearts. Earl Holt received an Army Commendation Medal. We thought we were getting Silver Stars like the other guys or maybe something even better. No other medals were awarded to us. After the ceremony, one of the other officers asked for my medal back, claiming they did not have enough Purple Hearts for the next group. I was only allowed to keep the certificate. All the soldiers getting awards knew each other, and I was the only person singled out. It was obvious that someone was getting even for my defiance. Purple Hearts have your name engraved on them. Who else is named Joseph Belardo in this unit? It probably got tossed in the shitter. My big mouth is always getting in the way.

February 27: Back at Dong Ha with another convoy, we heard they were serving steaks in the Battalion Mess Hall. We never had steaks where we lived. As we waited in a long line to get a hot meal, Dong Ha started getting hit by NVA artillery. Dong Ha had a loud alert siren and everybody ran into their bunkers for cover. The shells were landing by the airport about a half mile away. It was a rule in Dong Ha that you took cover when the siren blasted. My crew, who was used to being hit on the head by the shells, waited until the line of soldiers had taken cover. Once inside their Mess Hall, we loaded all their steaks and a few veggies into the insulated metal storage containers used to bring food to the men in the field. Hidden inside the Driver's compartment, we instantly took off for Carroll. When we returned, we shared our stolen treasurers with our friends. Steak never tasted so delicious.

March 1: Lt. Hardin informed us that he was restructuring our crew in preparation for Sam Lewis' return home. We would be individually assigned to other Dusters. To my surprise, Lt. Hardin made me the Squad Leader. I knew Sgt. Chester Sines and Sam Lewis had given him the recommendation. After a heated argument with the Lieutenant, I was allowed to keep Earl "Tex" Holt and train him as my Driver.

In the next few weeks, my crew constantly changed. I brazenly demanded to pick my crew from the new men arriving from Dong Ha.

March 2: Vince Tedesco has replaced Captain Easter as Charlie Battery's Commander. Tedesco took the time to visit and get acquainted with every Duster crew in our Battery. Instantly, we all liked this new Captain. All of us knew we finally had a great team leader. He recognized my crew from the awards ceremony and asked how we got wounded. When we told him we were the other Duster in the January 24th battle, he could not believe it. He looked stunned and amazed. He had heard rumors after the battle that there was another Duster in the battle, but no one seemed to be able to confirm the rumors. He had dismissed them, since he did not see us on the battle field, and was only instructed to retrieve the convoy, one tank and one Duster. Because of the awards ceremony, he knew we were wounded on the 24th but thought it was from another fire-fight. We exchanged stories of the battle. Each story filled the mental void of not knowing what really happened on the battlefield after we returned to Carroll.

March 3: Dusterman, Rodrigo Velazquez, was killed. I had only met him once, in Dong Ha.

March 4: I have been training Earl to be a Driver. He is a "natural" at it and got the feel of the Duster after only a few runs around the base. He only has one problem. He is slightly claustrophobic and got a little rattled when he had to crawl inside the hull of the Duster and practice retrieving ammo. I told him I had a simple remedy that would cure his nervousness. As he crawled into the bowels of the Duster to retrieve the last can of ammo, I had the guys quickly close the front door and hatch doors of the Driver's compartment and TC hatch. We then started pounding the sides of the Duster with hammers and fired off a few Duster rounds, simulating combat. After fifteen minutes, we opened up the doors and casually asked Earl if his claustrophobia was cured.

March 5: Tonight, we made camp with a platoon of Marines at the bottom of the hill below Carroll. Supposedly, we are some kind of blocking force. All we know is that we are again left as NVA bait and will be here for about a week. We are alone and isolated. We dug little one-man holes and used the dirt for our sandbags. It was better than nothing. I got tired of sleeping on the ground with the leeches and cockroaches. Our Duster made a run to the black market at Cam Lo. It was amazing what you could buy for an American dollar. We bought cots, sleeping bags, tarps, lawn chairs, and chaise lounges. We are now ready for upscale jungle-life living.

March 8: There were hundreds of dead NVA all along Route 9. You always don't have to see them. Your nose gives their positions away. The bodies turn almost black and swell like a helium balloon, moving as if alive from the maggots eating them. They finally burst and emit an odor that makes you want to throw up. I cannot believe how fast their bodies decomposed. Within a few weeks only their bones and a few clothes remained. It was a sight and smell beyond imagination. I hated running over them when we pulled off the main road.

March 14: We took Don Wolfe to the LZ on the south side of Camp Carroll where he waited for the chopper that would take him to Dong Ha. Don was going home. It was his last day in the 44th. We all wished him well and said the traditional "see ya later". It was getting harder to say good bye to my trusted old friends. Don was one of only a few men who would risk his life to save others. He had gotten wounded trying to save me and my crew. I didn't know how to thank him and just gave him a big hug. I had to compose myself as I turned away and waved goodbye.

As Don Wolfe's chopper lifted off of Camp Carroll, he could see the first of the NVA artillery shells hit Carroll.

I have just gotten a new Gunner, named Wally Owens, from Tennessee. He claims he has the eyes of an eagle and can shoot the balls off a monkey at two miles. Wally was being initiated into Charlie Battery with a fine meal from Camp Carroll's mess hall. As he gulped his first bite, I heard the popping sound of the NVA artillery shooting. Before anyone could hear the screaming and whistling sound of the NVA artillery shell flying through the air, the mess hall started to empty. By the time I grabbed Wally, we were the last to run out of the mess hall for cover. It was too late. As we dove threw the back mess hall door and hit the ground, the NVA artillery shells blew the mess hall in half. Fifteen more NVA shells were fired around the mess hall. Wally and I were really shaken-up. We never made the bunker and just hugged Mother Earth about ten feet from the mess hall. During the enemy artillery barrage, Doc Butler and Paul Conley ran around like crazy men helping all the wounded. Doc and Paul were two very brave people.

After the shelling and the smoke cleared, someone always yelled *"All Clear"*. I always wondered who the asshole was who decided it was ever *"All Clear"* in a combat zone. We began to scavenge for scraps of food, as we bitched at the NVA who had destroyed our beautiful mess hall. Our mess hall was the pride of "Artillery Hill."

Don later radioed me from Dong Ha to see who had got hurt and how bad the mess hall was hit. After a short conversation, we wished each other well and said our farewells.

Dear Diary

<u>On the Outside Looking In</u>

It seemed as a young man I had a special bond with nature. I spent hours exploring her, hiking her and enjoying her. She taught me to be patient, and my eyes and mind could and would be filled with her wonderment.

On the outside, I could look in and see her, like the song, beautiful and spacious skies, amber waves of grain, majestic mountains. I knew she had spread her grace on me.

I began to give my attention to others, by watching their eyes. Their eyes would tell all emotions.

I learned through eye contact, happiness, sadness, confusion, romance and love.

I experienced from the touch of the hand, the hug, that eye contact is what I thought a real man should be about.

Uncle Sam cast his eyes upon me and gave me the look of one of America's best. The new look fit me like a glove.

I enjoyed the hairy eyes the drill instructors could give. The stare-down the officers would try to show. I would return any look required. I knew sustained eye contact would give them away.

This Army Dog was now attached to the Halls of Montezuma. Like most GIs of my era, I was sent to the "Land of the Dragon"

My eyes could not believe her beauty. It was a feast for eye and mind. God didn't make this land for killing or dying, man did.

Uncle Sam sent me north to the ZEE. My eyes became filled with confusion.

I took on another new look, Squad Leader on a M42 Duster, a Twin 40 Millimeter Ack- Ack Gun.

It was our job to give the North Vietnamese Army the look of death. Something my eyes and mind had never seen or experienced.

The Duster separated men from man. There was no room to duck, no place to hide, nowhere to run. It was straightforward, face-to-face, eye-to-eye dueling; very little guessing of who was killing whom.

While the battles blazed, I could see from my open turret the Marines I supported. My eyes would agonize the feeling of others. Marines running, jumping, yelling, shouting, killing, screaming, wounded and dying. Arms, meant for hugging lovers, were now holding friends, wounded or dying.

All eyes now filled with horror, sorrow, fear, hate and pain.

...eyes screaming at each other for help.

...eyes looking for targets hiding in the shadows.

...eyes unbelieving.

...eyes fixed in stares, glazed by their final journey to their God.

I began to wonder, why my God allowed me to see these atrocities of life...these eyes of others.

The squeeze of the trigger was easy, but the eyes of the suffering and dead were forever

...regardless of who was on whose side.

I will go home a broken warrior.

Eyes and mind spent from too many firefights, too much Incoming.

Eyes being witness to the dark side of life.

My Uncle Sam had completed my training, eyes do tell all.

My eyes now walk this earth, half filled with tears.

Hoping never again to be "On the Outside Looking In".

March 21: Earl's case of Bibles has arrived. He was thrilled as we eagerly took the Bibles. We quickly stuffed them in all our jungle fatigue pants and jacket pockets, and thanked him for our extra Godly body armor. We needed all the protection we could get. Tex dropped to his knees and begged God to forgive us for our heathen ways. We still said our prayers with him nightly, holding our bibles tight.

March 25: Our crew had three Dusters destroyed by the NVA in a one-month period. We now hold the battalion record of five. God was with us again, none of us got a scratch, lots of tiny shrapnel splinters, but no real body damage. We are "Bodacious Bastards", the Marine tank retriever's number one customer. Our new Captain, Vincent Tedesco, sent Tex and me to Dong Ha to pick up another refurbished Duster. It was Earl's birthday and we celebrated the occasion with two cans of chili and beans, chased down with hot cocoa. I sang him a solo happy birthday song as he blew out a single candle (a match). It was Earl's well deserved few minutes of happiness.

I talked Earl into stealing the Colonel's prized toilet seat. As I played "chickie", Earl low crawled to the Colonel's shitter. It was the best thing we ever stole. When we got back to Carroll, Earl, on hearing that whoever stole the seat was going to get court-martialed, buried the seat in a place only he knew. He is a good Christian and prayed for forgiveness and our redemption.

At our 1990 DQS reunion at Fort Bliss, Texas, I called Colonel House and Earl Holt to the podium. I started telling the story of the Colonel's prized toilet seat. Members of the 1/44th cheered as I regaled them with the story of the precious white toilet seat. The Colonel started yelling. "I knew it was you, Belardo, I knew it was you." Earl had no idea I was going to do this and immediately started blaming me for the theft. It was hilarious. I casually presented the Colonel with a box. In it was a big white toilet seat and a piggy bank in the shape of a toilet with brass engraved plaques dedicated to the Colonel from Earl. I handed it to Earl and said "Earl you can now give the seat back to the Colonel. It's about time you got court-martialed." The place went wild as I held up my arms in victory.

To my surprise, the new Duster we got was one of my old tracks, C131, "The Track From Hell." This Duster has had more engines, transmissions, tension-bars, idler wheels and road wheels replaced than any other Duster in the Battalion. The track is full of bullet holes, dents, dings and two RPG holes in the lower chassis. Past crews joked about all the miles on it and that C131 saw more firefights than anything or anyone else did in Nam. Earl and I looked at each other, laughed, and said, "Wonder if the turret still jerks to the right when you shoot?" It still does.

In her future battles, the enemy would tattoo her beautiful green skin with two more RPG holes, twenty-three more bullet holes, and several more scratches and dents. Her battle scars were many, but we still loved her. This metal woman was still a born-again killer.

March 26: My crew now consists of Driver Earl Holt, Gunner Wally Owens, Cannoneers George Lewis and Benito Sitello. Earl is a big strong Texan over six feet, a kind, religious man whose faith always keeps him steady under fire, my second in command and my right hand man. We know each other well. Wally, a cigar smoking country boy, is steady and calm under fire and the best Gunner in the Battalion. He is always talking about fast cars and running moonshine. Benny is a Mexican who thinks he is Poncho Villa with his crisscrossed bandoleers and bad intentions. He keeps us serenaded us with his guitar, singing Spanish songs (Cielito Lindo being my favorite) with his fantastic falsetto voice. George, who everyone calls "Kung Fu George, is a big Californian, who carries a big 24 inch razor sharp Enfield Bayonet down the back of his flak jacket and is more than willing to demonstrate his martial arts and knife skills.

To my surprise and pleasure, they all rose above and beyond the call of duty. We were a team from the start. They easily learned each other's jobs. We trusted each other's judgment and fighting ability. Each of them possessed the right amount of courage and fear, a mixture in a man's soul that cannot be taught. I trusted them with my life, and they equally trusted me with theirs – a bond and friendship that will last forever.

Wally has the only set of hand-held hair clippers. All of our heads got their first good haircut. Wally should charge for his services; he would make a million. Grunts will buy anything and always need a trim.

Deep inside, I am proud to be their Squad Leader. They really know how to fight as a team. We give each other the needed confidence that each of us will make it home. My crew is unbelievably superstitious.

Again, they removed my "Grim Reaper" insignia from between the 40mm barrels. I just laughed and told them someday it would be back: ***We are the Grim Reapers.***

If we aren't doing convoys, we are doing search and destroy missions behind Carroll deep into the southwest, towards Khe Sanh. We continually see tracks from a suspected NVA PT76 Russian-made tank, which we hope our team will be the first to destroy.

Robert "Billy" Conley
Killed In Action February 1, 1968

Our Duster after it hit a land mine.

1st Sgt Alex Crawford

Camp Carroll Mess Hall blown up by NVA artillery.

Another destroyed Duster.

Left to right: George Lewis, Earl Holt, Wally Owens, and Melvin Hand.

The NVA road marker – symbolizing the savagery of the January 24th battle.

Proudly I stood (second from right), with a big smile, after being awarded the Purple Heart from Captain Vincent J. Tedesco.

CHAPTER 12: RELIEF FOR KHE SANH

March 27: Khe Sanh has been under siege by the NVA since around January 19th. The Khe Sanh area is now engaged in the largest battle we ever have had with the NVA. Our government does not want Khe Sanh to fall. The NVA has already attacked many American bases throughout Vietnam. The only success they achieved was with our newspapers and politicians. The enemy was beaten severely militarily, but that did not count. The newspapers still make us look like some losers. Thank God they did not report about WWII. We would be speaking another language. Why can't they tell the truth or at least back the soldier? We are trying to fight for another person's **Freedom**.

Our Duster was one of two Dusters assigned to meet the Army's 1st Cavalry Unit near Delta-5. The area they assembled in was a large, flat expanse of land we called the "Plains of Delta 5". It seemed like they had more equipment than all of the Third Marine Division. As the sun rose, we could smell food coming from their make-shift mess hall tent. I asked one of their officers if we could eat with their men. The officer rudely replied, "You live with the Marines, go eat with the Marines." I told the cocky Army bastard where to stick it and gave him the finger. I climbed up on the Duster and then pissed in his direction. The crew thought it was great and heckled him as we sat and ate our C-rations. We did our job and escorted the "Cav" up to Route 9 and west to Ca Lu, which was now being transformed into LZ Stud. Stud would be the jumping off point for Operation Pegasus. Pegasus was the name given to the reactionary forces assigned to reopen the road to Khe Sanh and relieve the troops stranded there.

We would fight alongside the Cav for a few days. It was slow going with a lot of shooting from our group and very little return fire from the enemy. I'm sure the Cav had some firefights up in the hill areas, but this particular group of the 1st Cav would brag how they saved the Marines from Dong Ha to Khe Sanh and how they kicked NVA ass. The NVA ass had already been kicked and beaten by hundreds of Marines, jets, and a million pounds of bombs dropped by the B-52s, and Dusters, Quad-

50s. On the whole, the resistance the NVA gave the Cav was minimal compared to the NVA's actual fighting abilities. That "minimal" gave the Cav a lot of trouble. Yes, they saw some action, but nothing like it was in the prior months. Yet the "Cav" always claimed bragging rights and that's okay. Even now, forty years later, they're still bragging.

April 4: LZ Stud was hit by 50 NVA artillery shells. Our job was to help the "Cav" open Route 9 from LZ Stud to Khe Sanh. I ***always*** thought they were supposed to be helping us. The going was slow and the fighting sporadic.

April 8: We finally rotated and got a rest. Our new position is back on top of Hill 250. I must have been back on someone's good list. If I could have chosen a place to spend my tour, it would be 250. Hill 250 is giving us a chance to regroup. But, we miss Roger's hot showers at The Water Point. The view from Hill 250 is magnificent. At daybreak, you stand above the low clouds, and as the mist lifts, you can see the horizon. It is breathtaking, and yet… it takes the breath away from the enemy because of the firing and shooting advantage from that hill. It is a shame how war mixes and twists our emotions… my emotions. I feel safe here, and that alone allows my brain and body to get much needed relaxation.

April 10: My crew got credited for shooting three NVA artillery rocket positions in three days. The secondary explosions were fantastic. We yelled with a madman's joy as the enemy positions were destroyed. Dead gooks meant no Marines would die that night. I enjoyed shooting the Marine .50 caliber sniper rifle from the lookout tower on top of 250. It was an awesome experience.

April 11: The Rockpile got hit by six NVA rockets. One of the rockets damaged a Duster and wounded one of the crew.

April 12: We were on a search and destroy mission with the Marines behind an old plantation slightly southwest of Delta-5. All of a sudden, 30 Viet Cong (VC) walked out of a tree line. They were all holding their hands and rifles high, yelling ***"Chieu Hoi – Chieu Hoi"*** (I surrender). We expected it to be some kind of trap. Almost all of them were dressed in their traditional daytime white pajamas. The Marines searched them and confiscated all their weapons and we marched them all to Delta-5. We kept them huddled in small groups outside of D-5. It was funny, because when we first radioed Carroll that we had captured 30 of the enemy, they thought we were joking and told us to shoot them. The leader of the VC constantly spoke and caused unrest among the prisoners and had to be separated from the other prisoners. We isolated him and had him stand tall at attention, with the Marines guarding him and orders to shoot if he moved. It took all day before some trucks finally arrived with an interpreter and took the VC away. I always wonder where they take all of the prisoners.

April 13: Along with the Cav, Larry Roundtree's Duster was one of two Dusters to be the first to drive into Khe Sanh after the 77 day siege.

April 14: Another 30 NVA rockets hit The Rockpile. One of our Dusters at The Rockpile spotted the NVA forward observer and hit him with a fast-eighty 40mm rounds. The NVA stopped shooting for the rest of the day.

We got a call on the lima-lima from Lt. Hardin, "Saddle up, you're going to rotate to Khe Sanh in the morning. We are relieving and replacing Duster "A" Battery who have survived the 77 Day Siege of Khe Sanh. Be at the main gate at 0600 hours." I was shocked when he told me to choose the other track that would be sent with me. To this Steve and I had gone from boot camp to Nam together. Steve might have never known it, but he was a courageous soldier and had a good crew. If the Khe Sanh I knew had changed like they said it had, Harris is my first choice. I also knew that Lt. Hardin would love to send Harris. A few weeks ago, Harris and Lt. Hardin had exchanged some serious words about an ambush they were in on the road to Khe Sanh. This was going to be a first; Dusters C131 and C132, sister tracks, would be together, defending one base.

Harris, who was stationed at the Khe Gio Bridge, seriously cut his foot while bathing in the river, and has been medivaced to Dong Ha. Another real good friend from boot camp, Frank Bardone, became acting Squad Leader. Bardone will take Harris' crew to Khe Sanh.

Steve was never told, and I mean never, that he was going to Khe Sanh. He wasn't even told that his track had left for Khe Sanh without him. Rumor had it he was really pissed when he got back to the Bridge and found that his track, complete with crew, was gone. I understand he got very upset with me when he was told I had volunteered him for Khe Sanh. What are friends for? It was a month before he caught up with his Duster. I was told they gave him KP and shit-burning details while he waited to catch a chopper to Khe Sanh. To this day I feel guilty for suggesting Steve Harris' track. I knew he would jump at the request, and he knew I would choose him.

April 15: We met Captain Vincent Tedesco, our new CO (Commanding Officer), at the main gate. He had never been to Khe Sanh and wanted to take the ride in his jeep, driven by his driver, Smitty. I looked around and saw no other vehicles or Marines. "Sir, are we waiting for the convoy to assemble?" "No Joe, we'll pick up the other Duster at the Khe Gio Bridge and then head out to Khe Sanh. Is that a problem?" "No, Sir." My crew looked at each other and smiled. We were not going with another convoy or the security of any other group, just three vehicles: Tedesco and his jeep driver, Smitty, Duster C132, and my Duster C131. Captain Tedesco is the best Commanding Officer we ever had at C-Battery. He leads us with courage and a true understanding of how the NVA fight and how to fight back. However, I thought driving to Khe Sanh with just three vehicles was a bit crazy. But, what the hell, you can't live forever! I am always comfortable when Tedesco is in charge. He treats all of the Duster and Quad crews with respect, asks for our advice and opinions, and listens to what we had learned in combat situations. The Captain and I hoped our little convoy would not become a casualty on the ride to Khe Sanh.

We were the first and, as far as I know, the only idiots ever to make a solo attempt to drive to Khe Sanh. Casually, we drove past The Rockpile, LZ Stud, Ca Lu and Joliet. We were about one third of the way to Khe Sanh when my engine blew. Black smoke was pouring out the engine grates. The Duster, known to be fast, was now reduced to a top speed of less than 5 miles per hour. Our track was now a great target for any decent NVA sniper, RPG team, or satchel charge thrower. We briefly stopped along the road to assess the damage. Tedesco informed us that he and the other Duster would proceed to Khe Sanh, with all due speed. If anything should happen, he would send help and return with all the Dusters and Quads at the base. Earl Holt, who never cursed or used God's name in vain, uttered his first words of profanity *under his breath.* Tedesco and Bardone departed for Khe Sanh, assuring us that we were great soldiers and knew how to fight, "You can just radio us for help." Bardone yelled, "Remember, we don't make house calls.

We waved goodbye to each other as the dust from the departing Duster hid us from view. Déjà vu of January 24th and other battles rushed through my brain. We even took pictures of their Duster as it sped down the road on the other side of the valley. I ordered my crew to unlock the turret, open the upper ammo boxes, slowly traverse back and forth, and stay extremely alert. I instructed Owens that, if shit happened, he was to shoot the first minute with both 40s on full auto as I swept the area. Cannoneer Lewis was to remain seated, holding four hand-grenades, ready to pull the pins and start throwing, before he started loading the 40s. The other Cannoneer, Sitello, was ordered to squat and use the M60 machine gun to cover the hill and cliff above our right side, and never stand up. All were instructed to keep a low profile and not talk, absolutely no talking. Talking to each other while on the road or during **"INCOMING!"** was something I absolutely forbid. All attention and concentration has to be on one's job, the enemy, and the direction of any enemy encounters. They are a great crew and knew what had to be done. It was routine business for Road Warriors. The balance of the ride to Khe Sanh seemed to take all day. *We all thanked God that nothing bad happened.* Over three hours alone on Route 9 to Khe Sanh was no place to be.

Years later, at a reunion, we joked with Tedesco and Bardone about how they left us on the road that day, and how Frank would not accept collect calls if we were attacked. I told them the only reason the NVA let them through was because they feared my Duster, The Grim Reaper. I guess we really were the only idiots to ever ride that section of road from Camp Carroll to Khe Sanh all alone and not get wounded or killed.

I had not been down the entire length of the road to Khe Sanh in many months. During Operation Pegasus, I could not believe how this once picturesque winding road had changed. The all out American push to save Khe Sanh had destroyed the area. The weeks of artillery, napalm and B-52 strikes had leveled everything. I told my men, ***"Welcome to Death Valley."*** Almost all the trees were gone or splintered, and the terrain looked like the earth was scorched and upside down. It made my hair stand on end. We had already chewed up Route 9 from Camp Carroll to Ca Lu. The area was filled with bomb craters, napalm scars, and dead NVA decaying along the sides of the road. The smell of death burned my nostrils and the rotting flesh upset my stomach. But this sight was like nothing I had ever seen. Our slow crawl to the infamous Khe Sanh changed our souls even more. None of us thought we would make it there alive and were relieved when we finally saw the main road leading into camp.

Our arrival at Khe Sanh turned into a bad omen for my superstitious crew. Captain Tedesco was with Bardone, having him take over the Duster position on the north side of the base at the east end of the runway by the old ammo dump. Our combat section from Charlie "C" Battery was relieving Alpha "A" Battery which was commanded by Lt. Bruce Geiger. "A" Battery had withstood the test of time during the infamous 77 day siege. Tedesco went back to Dong Ha escorted by Larry Roundtree's Duster, the two Dusters from Alpha Battery, and two Quad 50s, one of which was being towed. Also accompanying them was a convoy of Marines.

Our new position was the bunker at the northwest end of the runway across from "Charlie Med.". The "A" Battery Duster was pulling out of the parapet as we arrived. They expressed their joy about leaving. Two Marines, waving goodbye to them, stood in the mouth of the track's three-sided parapet which was next to our new bunker position. The NVA opened up with a barrage of artillery from Co Roc, a mountain enemy fortification in Laos a few miles away. The first shell was a direct hit on the two Marines. We never heard it coming. They were blown to smithereens. Parts of them were scattered all over our parapet, bunker, and Duster. As the enemy artillery rained down on the base, Tedesco and the convoy left as quickly as possible. We helped the Marines quickly bag as many parts of their comrades as we could find, and ran them across the runway to Graves Registration.

Our new position was still covered with the remains and blood of the two unfortunate Marines. My crew stood there in disbelief. Nobody had ever been killed right next to our bunker. Being killed twenty feet away was okay, one hundred feet away was even better. For some strange reason, anyway or anywhere you died on the road was okay and understandable. We had seen death many times and knew all about dying and suffering and picking up the pieces. But this, a direct artillery hit on a fellow American next to what was our private sanctuary, our bunker, our home, was totally unacceptable. It happened so fast; there was no time to take cover. We did not have time to close our eyes or blink. We just watched in total disbelief.

My crew had done their fair share of what we called "being smoked," a term we used when the 40mm cannon shell hit an NVA soldier. When one of ours got "smoked," it had a whole new meaning. My men would remember this day forever. On our Duster we carried rakes, picks and shovels. As my crew checked out their new bunker, I hastily raked the rest of the Marines' remains into a pile. I then shoveled the pile into an old rusty half of a 55 gallon drum. I had the crew carry the drum about a one hundred feet west of our bunker. I then shoveled dirt on all the blood stained ground around our area. Holt backed up the Duster into the parapet. We were now ready for the NVA. As a team, we quickly finished our task of *"it's only a thing"* and went back to business. After we were settled into our bunker, I burned the remains in the drum.

As the ashes rose, Earl walked over and read from *"the Good Book"*. The five of us huddled together around the drum to give a final salute to America's best. The words of God took the mental edge off what now had turned into a very bad day. Unbelievably, we stood there, stoically, while the billowing smoke allowed the NVA to hone in on our position. Bombs began bursting around us, but nothing or no one could or would interfere with our ceremony. At the end of our ceremony, we casually walked back and entered our new home.

We would find parts from those Marines until we left Khe Sanh. The drum would become our area's crematorium for all the body parts that never made the body bags. We hoped the NVA artillery would not hit our crematorium and kill more of our friends. Empty boots, pairs or singles, some whole, some in pieces would stand guard duty at our crematorium. Body parts were added daily. Earl's words from the Bible continually healed our fragile souls.

Dear Diary:

FEAR

Nam, where lives are lost and saved everyday without thought of its psychological consequence.

I remember the many days of being shot at and the sight and inner fear of seeing a friend shot or dead. Bullets are like something reaching for me, unseen, but heard, unbiased and deadly.

My mind cannot grasp the swift change of events in an all out fire-fight. My trained reflexes have me running, dodging, hiding and returning fire.

The shadow of death is all around me. The sounds of war, the suffering, the dying, is in itself...unbelievable.

The fear of perishing, that struggle for self-preservation, keeps me going. It was just like they said it would be, all blood and guts. The only thing they left out was John Wayne.

The military could train me for just about anything, except the harassment and interdiction of artillery warfare. It was like nothing I could imagine. The sound alone made my heart stop. I can only relate to this by having you lie between railroad tracks and have the Baltimore Express pass over you.

One artillery shell fired at you isn't too bad. It only lasts for a few seconds and only hits one spot. When the barrage begins, the destruction is devastating. The long lasting artillery attack plays havoc with my mind. If I'm caught in the open, I'm scrambling for the nearest shelter, preferably a bunker. Once inside I'm still not safe. All I have accomplished is the elimination of a lot of shrapnel. We just sit and wait in huddled masses. Listening, wondering, waiting for the one with your name on it. That endless time, working on your nerves. Minutes seem like hours, hours feel like days. Screams from the wounded, sighs of the dying, the helping that never seems to be enough.

I begin to wander, dreaming of home, my loved ones and the things we haven't done, but want to. I begin to pray, praying silently, praying in groups.

Fear has come a-calling and I have to suck up all that is holy to me, all that has made me what I am, all that will show the men around me that I will get them though this and send them home in one piece.

Like the scream of a murdered woman, a shell lands close and reawakens me to my surroundings. A twelve-foot cube, seventeen feet below Mother Earth, totally in darkness.

Finally it's quiet and we crawl from the bowels, the womb of our Mother, exhausted from mental fatigue.

"Thank God I'm alive."

April 19: A Convoy heading to Khe Sanh with Marine Unit G-2/9 was ambushed by the NVA. Dusters provided direct fire support on NVA main positions, enabling the Marines to extract their wounded and dead. Four Dustermen were wounded in action protecting the Marines.

My crew and I hate Khe Sanh. It is a stagnant position and we are road warriors. The siege is over, except for a few snipers that are always trying to kill us. The **"INCOMING!"** never stops, and the big guns from Co Roc, Laos, never stop pounding the base at will. Hundreds of enemy artillery shells hit the base daily. Living conditions are deplorable. The NVA has blown the base into little pieces. Garbage and debris are strewn all over the place. The only true things that rule the base were the rats. The rats are as big as rabbits. They grow larger by the day as they feast on the dead NVA in **Death Valley**. We share our bunker with families of rats. A rat crawling on you during your sleep is an everyday common occurrence. Often, a rat sits next to you while you eat your C-rations or write a letter home.

April 25: We have inherited a dog, or should I say a puppy, named "Rex" from a Marine named Bruce. The dog's name was instantly changed to Comanche, the handle given to Dusters from Charlie Battery. The dog breaks the monotony of the constant **"INCOMING!"** and that lonely isolated feeling. He is a good dog and is the mascot of everyone on the northwest end of the runway. Today, Comanche started frothing at the mouth and shaking. We feared he might have rabies. He is still just a pup and likes to gnaw on our fingers. Panic set in. We all thought we had rabies. Rabies meant getting two weeks of shots in your belly, something we all dreaded. We preferred fighting the NVA rather than dying from rabies.

April 27: I came up with this great idea and gave the dog a name, Pvt. Charles Comanche. On the next medivac chopper, we sent George Lewis and Pvt. Comanche to the hospital in Da Nang. We knew George would find a doctor to treat our dog. Avoiding rabbi shots in all our bellies depended on him. Comanche was diagnosed with distemper and was sadly put to sleep.

George was no fool and stayed a few extra days at China Beach. He claimed he could not get back to Khe Sanh. His stories about the USO show were refreshing. We were all jealous.

April 29: Our new Lt., who we call Lieutenant Dan, has arrived. He took up position at the other end of the runway just past the Quad-50s. The Lieutenant doesn't even know George and, therefore, doesn't know that he is gone. Captain Tedesco has placed me in charge of the Dusters and the two Quad-50s. The poor Lt. is new and the guys just nod their agreement to his instructions and then ask me if his instructions are correct.

It was a very long, life-threatening trek between Dusters, a journey the Lt. seldom made. When he did come, he had collected an assortment of strange souvenirs along the way and sent them back to Camp Carroll on the next convoy.

1st Cavalry, U.S. Army, assembling on the plains of Delta – 5 for Operation Pegasus.

1st Cavalry practicing opening and closing their portable bridge.

*Escorting the convoy for Operation Pegasus past the Khe Gio bridge
outpost area, then to The Rockpile through Ambush Alley to LZ Stud.*

*In the convoy the Dusters had the big 175mm cannons of the 2nd/94th Artillery.
The Dusters dropped off the cannons at The Rockpile.*

213

Quad-50's covering the rear section of the convoy.

*175mm Gun shooting from The Rockpile
in support of Khe Sanh during Operation Pegasus.*

Marines waiting to be loaded on CH34's for Operation Pegasus.

Frank Bardone's Duster and crew as they head to Khe Sanh,
leaving us behind and alone on Route 9.

"Death Valley" section of Route 9.
It was an area decimated by American artillery, jets, and B-52 bombers.
This eerie place smelled of death and made our hair stand on end.

There were thousands of B-52 bomb craters along Route 9
and in the valleys leading to Khe Sanh.

In Vietnam - church was where the Chaplain stood.
His alter a pile of sandbags.

The washed out bridge area leading to Khe Sanh called the "Hair Pin."

A view of Khe Sanh at the west end.

Aerial view of Khe Sanh. Our Duster was in the lower right of the photo, to the left of the runway's square end on the base perimeter.

Khe Sanh Hill Fights

The number of the "Hill"
represents the hill elevation in meters above sea level

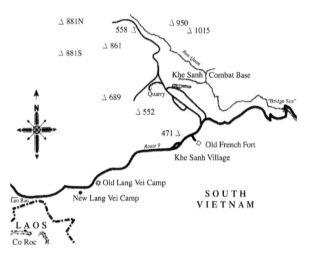

Khe Sanh Combat Base

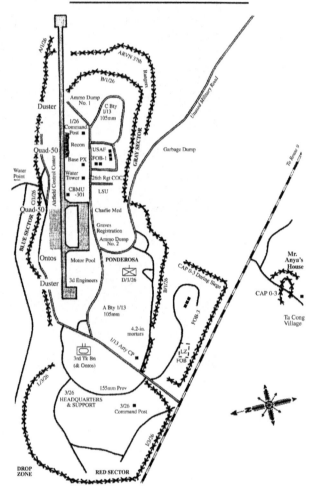

CHAPTER 13: ABANDONING KHE SANH

May 2: To break the monotony, we are always playing jokes on each other – Army versus Marines. I caught another rat, a nice big two pounder. My crew helped me tie a long rag to the rat's tail. Just before it got dark, we doused the rag with gasoline, lit it on fire and dropped it in the long trench that went around Khe Sanh. Like a flaming bottle rocket, the rat ran down the trench. The Marines, thinking that some tiny flaming gook was running at them, jump out of the trench, screaming and shooting at the rat.

May 4: The Marines got even today and threw a teargas grenade into our bunker. Choking, coughing, gagging, with saliva drooling out of our mouths and snot running out of our noses, we crawled out of our bunker. Our friendly Marines cheered with joy at their victorious payback.

It took about a week for the teargas to disappear. We had no windows to open and only one doorway into the bunker. Since teargas is heavy, it clung to our underground bunker. It was the only time I used my gas mask.

May 8: The NVA artillery from Co Roc seems endless. Huddled in our bunkers, we just take all they can give. After it subsides, we check our area for any wounded or dead. Today, we found two dead black guys, blown to shreds. I told the guys in the area we had to gather them up and bring them to Graves Registration. We only had two ponchos in which to put them. Leaving them with their assignment, I continued on my mission checking out the area. On my return, the men were just finishing up their gruesome task. In their haste to rebuild these two guys into human shapes, they inadvertently mixed parts. One guy was a very light skinned black, maybe even Spanish, and the other guy was very dark. They looked at me in horror when I instructed them to rebuild them properly. ***"They Have Mothers."***

May 10: I played with a rat I trapped under one of the empty ammo cans. Using the asbestos gloves from the Duster, I tied a wire around the rat's body and then attached a piece of parachute cord to the wire. I then tied my little harnessed friend to a long stick. You should have seen everybody jump when I walked past them with my pet rat.

May 14: Dusterman Jose Diaz was killed today.

May 17: It has been well over a month since our last shower, and sponge baths are few and far between. Earl noticed a gross-looking giant blackhead sticking out of Wally's ear. Instantly, Earl wanted it removed and Wally was not in agreement. George, now in on the removal idea, started chasing Wally all around the base with Earl in hot pursuit, screaming "C'mon Wally, it won't hurt, it'll be a cinch! We're just going to do a little **surgery!** After what seemed like a hundred yard chase, Wally was finally tackled and dragged back to our bunker area. There they were, two big guys, pinning poor Wally to the ground. Earl was sitting on his chest, pinning his shoulders down, and George was kneeling on his head so Earl could get a good look in the ear. Like crazed men in a fox hunt, they pulled out their bayonets and told Wally they were going to cut that disgusting thing out of his ear. Wally was kicking and screaming, thinking they would cut off his ear. Agreeing that the bayonets were too big, they decided to use two big ten-penny nails, using them like giant tweezers. After a lot of screaming, the two held up their prized piece of surgery, stuck to the end of one of the nails. They then proceeded to pour surgical alcohol in Wally's ear, announcing "Now it won't get infected." **Poor Wally...**

May 20: I got a call on the radio. It was Tank. Casually, as if it were a Sunday phone call, his voice chirped with enthusiasm "Joey, this is John Huelsenbeck and I'm going home." We both screamed with joy. John had done his year in Hell. I was happy for him and yet sad that he was going home. We had become great friends and had gone through a lot of terrifying, horrible shit together. John is one of the bravest men I have ever met and I respect him to the utmost. When he was with you, you knew your back was being covered. It gave me and the rest of the men a comfortable feeling. I don't think there's another soldier or

Marine on the DMZ who can fill John's shoes. I owed my life to this man and prayed he would get home safely.

May 22: Khe Sanh has removed what little was left of our shame and modesty. The constant **"INCOMING!"** has blown up almost all the shitters. The empty 40mm cans have become our depositories. The cans, filled with a little kerosene, were placed in the trenches or brought into the bunkers. God, it is embarrassing. The airtight lids keep the smell down. It is only bad when in use. Burning shitters at Khe Sanh has become a no-no. The NVA can see the burning shit smoke for miles and *will* put an artillery shell on top of you as you take a crap, a mess that nobody treasures cleaning. Anywhere from five to sixteen guys are crammed into our twelve foot cube bunker. We made bunk beds from old scraps of wood and used an old M-16 ammo can converted into gasoline lantern as light. Opening the 40mm can and taking a shit in the center of our bunker is a nightmare. Jokes are endless, toilet paper is rationed. When the bunker is full of guys, the guy taking the dump is shown no mercy. Nothing is sacred. We all laugh and it relieves the cruelty of war, if even for a moment.

May 24: Our Duster still has a bad engine and is used only to retrieve recon teams and Marines close to our perimeter. I guess that is good for us, because we can't do convoys, mine sweeps, or search and destroys.

Instead, we have other tasks such as digging out the wounded and dead out from the bunkers hit by the NVA artillery. Hoping to hear sounds of life, we dig feverously with our hands. We can't use shovels and picks because they will cut up or kill the friends you are trying to save. The constant body recovery has fried our brains and gives a whole new meaning to brotherhood.

May 25: Water is a prized commodity at the base and we are unable to get our own water, so I got the idea to build a shower. The guys thought I was crazy because we didn't have enough drinking water, no less shower water. We had been taking little baths out of our helmets. I had them cut the lid off an old Agent Orange drum and clean the inside out with rags and dirt. They then put a hand release fire hose nozzle in the drum's small screw hole. We wedged the drum on top of the bunker and announced to the Marines that we had a shower. My plan is to make a deal with the Marine Lt. who is in charge of the Marines who live in the trenches on our north perimeter. We will provide showers for all his men, if he supplies us with water.

He agreed. Our position, thereafter, always had water, thanks to our shower. We used our gasoline pump to draw the water up into the drum. It was great while it lasted.

May 26: We had been ordered to abandon the KHE SANH COMBAT BASE. This was something we thought would never happen. This must have been another one of Robert McNamara's brilliant ideas. We had kicked NVA ass all over the DMZ. We were winning the war. The troops thought it was time to keep the ground for which we fought and march on Hanoi. Abandoning this base would destroy all the reasons we had fought. It was political suicide and the warrior did not count. So many Americans had died in vain. So many Americans were severely wounded, both physically and mentally. We all knew it was the turning point of the war. Even though I do not like the war, it is not in my mental makeup to give up, quit, retreat, or lose at anything that costs lives. The warrior in me will rise to the occasion, step to the front of the line, face my adversaries head on, and be mentally and physically accountable.

**** Abandoning Khe Sanh was a personal insult to all Vietnam Veterans ****

May 28: One of the other items we never have enough of is C-rations. Our convoys bring us ammo and mail, but always seem to forget to bring rations on their weekly jaunts. I have lost another thirty pounds during my stay at Khe Sanh. I now weigh around 145 pounds and have lost over 60 pounds since I had arrived in Nam. We started to monitor the helicopter drops each evening at our end of the runway. Tonight, after the chopper was gone, Gary Dahlheimer's Marine Ontos crew and my crew raided the shipment. Our stretcher was used to carry off all usable items and food. This, our best raid yet, yielded dehydrated hamburgers. They looked like little gray cardboard squares. We placed them in our mess kit frying pan, added water and a little heat from C-4 *--Ole' hamburgers!* Gary opened a big can of string beans and we all ate like kings.

May 29: It is like the original 77-day siege has never ended. The NVA continually pound the base with heavy artillery. I stopped counting incoming at 250. My brain is beginning to falter. I am losing track of time and dates. I really don't give a shit. I walk the area tall and proud, defying the snipers. My men don't question me.

May 30: The convoy brought me an extra man named Simon. Benny, my Cannoneer, will take Simon under his wing and teach him what is expected and what was happening at this base.

Lt. Dan told me that I was going on R&R to Formosa for five days. I told him I didn't want to go because I was waiting for an opening to go to Australia.

June 1: Before I could fill two sandbags, I found myself landing in Formosa. Bruce, the Marine who gave us the dog, was on the same plane and the two of us teamed up together.

June 6: Bruce and I had partied for five days. The head cook and manager at the hotel had gone to school at New York University. It was like old home week for me, since I came from New Jersey. Bruce and I drank and ate like it was our last meal. We got so drunk that they had to drag us to our rooms. I guess somewhere in one of our drunken stupors we got a haircut and a manicure. As Bruce and I sat in the hotel lobby, I noticed something shiny on my fingernails. Still drunk, it took me a while to realize someone had put clear nail polish on our fingers. Bruce and I started laughing our asses off. Stumbling and crawling, we made our way back to the hotel barber (a woman) and had her remove the polish. God, what would the guys back at Khe Sanh think?

June 7: Bruce and I returned to Khe Sanh. Bruce asked me to hold his Yashica camera and take care of his personals while he went on patrol.

Bruce never returned. I will always miss his crazy laugh and stupid jokes. I still have his camera.

June 8: To amuse ourselves, we have wrestling and boxing matches with the other Duster crews who come in on the convoys from LZ Stud. Our crew, because of our bad ass Kung Fu Master George Lewis, is always the winner. Occasionally, we even have a rock throwing fight. We are totally nuts. Yesterday, I got hit in the face with a big rock and now have a giant black eye. Captain Tedesco arrived out of nowhere on the next convoy. I think he came just to bust my balls and tease me. "Belardo, I heard how you got that black eye, and you're not getting another Purple Heart," the Captain bellowed. My crew thought this was great. We could have all been dead and the Command would not have known or possibly even given a shit. Get whacked in the head with a rock and the whole DMZ knew about it. I was known to have handed out a few black eyes. This must have been God's way of getting even. The joke was on me and that was okay.

June 9: Dusterman Manuel Martinez from Alpha Battery, who survived the 77 Day Siege of Khe Sanh, was killed today.

We all feel guilty that our brothers-in-arms from the 3rd Marine Tanks were killed just outside the gates of Khe Sanh. Marine Sgt. Clifford Evans was killed. He was one of our best friends. I had fought a lot of battles with him on that "Road to Hell". Our engine is now almost completely dead. If they had replaced our engine in a timely fashion, we might have been able to help or save them. Cries for help on the radio will ever haunt me. We questioned everyone, over and over, if they were sure Evans was dead.

June 10: The new guy Simon has rubbed everyone the wrong way. We had a C-ration policy that each person on the crew took turns eating the famous beanie weenies. Simon was left alone today to guard the bunker while our Duster went to the other end of the camp to shoot at a suspected NVA position. After our return, George Lewis discovered that Simon had eaten his beanie weenies. George is a very large, very strong man, much larger than Simon and a Kung Fu Master to boot. He is truly a real badass man, not someone you want to piss off. George, who carries an old razor sharp "Enfield Bayonet" strapped to the back of his flak jacket, took it out and wanted to carve up Simon. It was amazing how a simple can of food could make a man crack. Simon thought it was a joke, but George went ballistic. If I could not calm George down, Simon was going to die. I had never seen George get so angry with anyone about anything. Simon had crossed the wrong bounds and broken crew trust. Trust in each other is the only thing we have to offer. It is sacred to my men. To appease George and the rest of the crew, I ordered Simon to cover our bunker with a new layer of sandbags. Simon filled, tied, and stacked every sandbag by himself, with George as his personal watchdog.

June 11: I explained the situation to our Lieutenant, and about my fear for Simon's safety. He agreed with my concern and will send Simon back to Camp Carroll on the next convoy.

June 13: The convoy from Carroll was scheduled to arrive at noon. Simon was leaving us but, before he left, I made him empty all the sand bags he had filled, plus a few hundred more. We were taking Khe Sanh apart. Plus, no one fucks with my crew.

June 14: A Douglas A4 fighter plane from one of the aircraft carriers signaled *"Mayday"* to the base, indicating that it must attempt an emergency landing on Khe Sanh's short runway. The edges of the runway were already filled with planes and helicopters destroyed during the siege and since our arrival. The base came alive. Men scurried from their holes to get a better look at what might be added to the collection of relics along the runway. Poised with shovels, fire extinguishers, stretchers, and water, we waited with cameras around our necks for the jet's arrival. It was the most excitement we have had since the chopper had left dehydrated hamburgers and grapefruits on the runway for us to steal.

The A4 plane landed with its brakes locked and engines in full reverse thrust. It came to a screeching halt a few feet short of the end of the runway. Everyone ran to its aid. The pilot was a little shaken, but seemed to be in good health. The jet had a small hole in its fuel tank and had run out of gas. The pilot was lucky that the plane's tail hook didn't catch on something as he came down the runway. We were all fortunate that the NVA were not shooting at the base from Co Roc. The fighter plane was dragged off the runway and into an old helicopter revetment for protection.

June 16: This day, the A4 was dragged out from the protection of the revetment and positioned on the end of the runway. With his plane's gas tank repaired and its tail hook strapped to the fuselage, the pilot was eager to take off. As the pilot got into the cockpit, he gave all of us the "High Sign." The "thumbs up" gesture made us all start cheering. We all waved and screamed as the jet roared down the runway, lifted, and was gone from our sight. Minutes later, the pilot flew the jet a few hundred feet over the base, doing victory rolls and spiraling into the sky. It was a good day for all. The monotony was broken with joy and excitement, and no one was injured.

June 19: Eric Metler, one of the mechanics from Camp Carroll, arrived on the morning's convoy, riding shot-gun on the boom-truck with a Duster engine strapped to the deck for our Duster. It was like every NVA artillery piece in the area took aim on his truck and our new engine. We already had prepared for our engine's removal and had disconnected all the connections. I think it was the first time in Duster history that an engine was removed and installed during an enemy artillery barrage. As the driver raised the boom higher to remove the old engine, it acted like a homing device for the enemy artillery. The exploding bombs covered us in hot shrapnel and earth. I felt sorry for Eric, the truck driver, and my crew, but the convoy was only staying for an hour or two and the engines must be swapped. My crew finished the final assembly after the convoy left. I never heard a Duster crew pray and curse out a Duster engine in the same breath. Eric was thrilled when he finally left Khe Sanh. He didn't even wave goodbye. It was great to have Grim Reaper running again.

June 21: I celebrated my twenty-first birthday today. Eric had brought me a care package from my family and girlfriend. They sent me cookies, popcorn, pepperoni and provolone cheese. All of us thought we were at a feast as we celebrated my passage into manhood. I cannot remember when the actual passage took place. It must have happened between the enemy artillery explosions. We ended our feast with our favorite meal from home, Lucky Leaf Baked Apples in a can. I carefully cut each apple so that each of us got the same size piece. We then drank the syrup a spoonful at a time. We finished our delicacy with each of us taking turns putting our tongue in the can and getting those last tasty licks.

June 22: We have been having trouble with a helicopter pilot and crew who get their kicks hovering over our position and causing a dust bowl. This helicopter arrives twice a day to pick up Marines leaving the base. The pilot hovers a few feet over our bunker and has his door gunner point his gun at my men. The red clay dust clung to the oiled 40mm cannons. They make so much dust that we have to re-clean the guns every time he comes. We do not want them to jam when fired.

June 23: I met the helicopter at the runway and advised the pilot that his intentional dusting had to stop. The pilot was an arrogant bastard with a severe attitude problem and told me where to shove it. I told him it wasn't a game and I would love to kick his ass, and that my men would love to shoot his mangy butt out of the sky.

June 24: Today, the same asshole helicopter pilot repeated his routine. As the helicopter was hovering over us, we heard a loud popping noise, and the chopper burst into flames. It crashed just outside our perimeter wire. We ran out and saved the mangy bastard, his crew, and passengers. They were lucky only to have some broken noses and minor cuts.

June 25: A group of officers showed up at our bunker today and accused us of shooting the helicopter out of the sky. I laughed and advised them that if we had shot them, they all would be dead. I told them they should go check out the helicopter. It was located on the other side of the wire and visible from the perimeter. I told the questioning Colonel that they should give us a medal for saving their sorry asses. *We were never questioned again.*

June 26: I got hit in the left shin with shrapnel. A long piece of thin shrapnel was sticking out my pant leg. I reported to what was left of the aid station, Charlie Med, across the runway from our bunker. I was not questioned as to who I was or what unit I was with and the Marine doctor quickly treated me. After viewing all the Marines with much more serious wounds, I was overcome with shame for seeking treatment for my nicked shin. I spent the next couple of hours assisting as a stretcher-bearer for the wounded and the dead.

June 27: My crew and I helped out at Charlie Med and Graves Registration, a poignant reminder of the small price I have paid compared to so many others. Stretchers, carrying the wounded and the dead, are a daily vigil. My crew helps the Corpsmen with the wounded, separating them in accordance with the severity of their wounds. For moral purposes, those dying are moved away from the aid station and given morphine to ease their suffering. I help administer the morphine shots. When needed, we help Graves Registration clean and care for the dead. We clean their faces, or what is left of their faces, before we load them onto outgoing choppers. It is the least we can do for their mothers. Sometimes the whole crew helps. We called this detail "Cleaning Faces," an ordeal of mixed emotions that, I am sure, will haunt me a lifetime.

Months later, a small rusty spot appeared on my left shin from the shrapnel. It's been over forty years and the rusty spot still appears. Putting on my socks each day is a daily reminder of my stay at Khe Sanh.

June 28: My crew did not get upset when they found out I had added the symbol of the Grim Reaper back on the front gunplate. I had upgraded from my skull painting to a real NVA skull. The hardships of war had collapsed my moral fibers and my Christian upbringing, plus NVA bones were everywhere. To my surprise, the crew thought this was the greatest. They nicknamed the skull "Ho Chi." Kissing their first two fingers, they each took turns patting the skull for good luck. By now we speak openly of never going back to the real world. Nam is now our home and this is where we will die. My crew and I have crossed over to the dark side of life. It is becoming hard to focus on anything nice or anything real. If it wasn't for our CARE packages, perfumed letters from home, and mail call, I think we would have totally flipped by now.

June 29: As instructed, without haste, we continue to dismantle the base. I had been put in charge of our area and was told not to leave anything standing. All trenches and foxholes were to be filled. All buildings, bunkers and shelters were to be torn down. If we cannot take them down, we were to blow them up. Nothing, not even the garbage, will be left for the NVA. Our bunker and the Ontos crew's bunker next to us will be the last to be destroyed. These bunkers will be used to shelter the remaining clean-up crews from the enemy artillery.

The NVA snipers never stop shooting and the NVA artillery from Co Roc increased their fire missions to well over 300 rounds a day. As trenches and bunkers disappear, our living conditions have become a nightmare. As far as we are concerned, the "Siege" is still on. Hundreds of enemy artillery shells hammer us twenty-four hours a day. I stop counting each time when the hundredth round hits. We strip all the bunkers of their sandbags. As the sandbags are removed, we cut them open and dump out the earth. All metal roof decking, ammo cans and empty brass used for roof artillery deflecting material are gathered, loaded on trucks, and shipped off the base. We use the Dusters to pull the big roof timbers out of the bunkers. Bulldozers fill the empty bunker holes and the area is leveled.

My men and the Marines continually scamper into the few remaining small holes and trenches trying to stay alive. The rats scurry over the debris, men search for cover and their own place to live or die. Rats, our other enemy, have become comrades trying to stay alive. When we awake each morning, there is always a family of rats huddled against us, seeking our body warmth for comfort. We just look at each other, their little red eyes staring at us for help and food. Each morning I yell "Good Morning, Mr. Rat." "Good Morning, Mr. Belardo." "If you get any bigger I might just eat you." Living under the Dusters has become home to the Marines. The enemy knows we are abandoning Khe Sanh. Some **asshole reporter** had it plastered all over the front pages of every newspaper in the world. **The press has gotten a lot of great young Americans killed.** The enemy continues to increase their daily artillery barrages on the base. Now I stop counting at three hundred. The NVA shelling is unbelievable, killing and severely wounding many of the Marines who live in shallow shelter holes they had dug in front of our Duster. There is no safe place to hide. We stack the dead and wounded by the old "Charlie Med." A small group of Corpsmen assist those brought to this area the best they can. Convoys and helicopters come and go on a daily basis.

June 30: Khe Sanh has all but vanished before our very eyes. We didn't waste time and leveled the Ontos' bunker with the use of C-4 explosives. **"INCOMING!"** was fierce. We took cover in our bunker, the last full standing fortification. As we crowded in this 12 foot cube, 17 feet underground, an enemy artillery shell hit. The bunker buster round exploded and collapsed the left rear corner of the bunker, burying Wally and me alive. The only thing that kept us alive and from being crushed to death was the homemade bunk beds we took cover under. It took the guys about twenty hours to dig us out. When you dig for men, you dig slowly so you don't cut them in half with the shovels and picks. It took hours for them to clear the sandbags, ammo cans, old 40mm brass, and runway matting off our bunker. Wally was lucky and only had small cuts and lots of black and blues. My left leg had been partially pulled out of its hip socket and had turned purple, red and blue. I must have been in shock because it didn't hurt and I don't remember much. At the aid station, the guys held me down as the Doc pulled my leg back into place. It hurt like hell and I passed out. The good old Doc gave me a bottle of that military cure all-pill, the APC's (all purpose capsule – aspirins), and sent me back to my position. Mother Earth under the Duster had become our home. I watched as my men slowly removed about five feet off the remaining top portion of our bunker. Hundreds of enemy artillery shells pounded the area around our position. Hell would be a better place to live. My men slept in the fetal position as if hoping to return to the womb and get a new chance at life. I couldn't take it anymore, went back to work and ordered the bunker to be leveled by C-4. I don't want any more of my men to die from exposure to the enemy artillery. We all prayed with Earl.

Now, years later, I suffer from circulation damage, a bad back, and numb legs due to this incident.

July 2: The only thing we left was the three-sided earthen parapet for the Dusters, Quad-50s, and Ontos. We slowly moved our clean-up crew toward the east end of the runway. Our Duster accompanied us as a portable artillery shelter and bunker. We eventually rendezvoused with Steve Harris's crew at the other end of the runway. Most of the Marines have already been evacuated from the base. Our Duster crews and a hand full of Marines guarded the entire length of the north side of the old runway area. It is July 2nd and the mighty Khe Sanh is no more, reduced to a flat plateau with a small group of America's Best guarding her virtues.

July 3: I do not want the NVA artillery getting a fix on us, so we frequently move the Duster to different locations around the base. The biggest targets left standing on the base are our Dusters, giant silhouettes on a barren plain. Each evening, to keep the NVA in check, we continue the Vietnam tradition of shooting from the camp perimeter. Some call it "Mad Minutes". I call it "Moments of Madness". The Twin 40s clear the perimeter nightly of any NVA, hoping to get close to the base until we can leave for good.

July 4: The day we celebrate Old Glory was spent watching the choppers speed across the base, trailing different colored smoke grenades. This is hopefully our last night at the infamous base. The NVA, who always seemed to have good intelligence, knew this could be their last chance to shoot at Khe Sanh.

*The constant "**INCOMING!**" had, without my knowledge, fried my brain. July 4th now takes on a whole new meaning. Fourth of July fireworks have become my "Achilles 'heel".*

*My family and friends joke at my involuntary twitching and my fast departure from our country's yearly display of freedom. My family thinks it's the explosion of the fireworks that makes me anxious. I try to explain to them that fireworks are like Dusters shooting. The attack starts real slow, a few bursts here and a few there. There are lots of white flashing and sparkling lights, as if the enemy is probing the wire and we're popping illumination flares with smoke trails floating away in the breeze. Then come a few bigger explosions, and then a few more, followed by lots of whistling ones and colorful ones. A noise rises from the crowd, screaming their "oohs" and "aahs". Explosion after explosion, momentum builds and builds, to the Grand Finale. Then comes the final push from the enemy, a human wave rushing at you, with guns blazing as if they were special ground effects. The crew of the Duster, holding fast in their turret, waiting, waiting, waiting, anticipating that terrifying moment, the heart stopper of every battle when someone screams **"Enemy In The Wire!"** The Duster, on full auto-fire, becomes the Grand Finale, shooting 240 high-explosive cannon shells a minute point blank at the advancing enemy, producing a kaleidoscope of exploding colors with deadly intentions. Ripping the enemy to shreds, like giant red, yellow and green fluorescent paintballs, each round is followed to its target by a sparkling burning tracer of death in its tail. Explosion after explosion can be heard, followed by the roar of war - giving witness to your day of killing. Like the 4th of July, it ends as fast as it started and the only thing left is the smell of sulfur and that quiet hazy calm.*

July 5: Marine Unit 2/1 departed Khe Sanh in the middle of the night. I was shocked when I checked the perimeter and found no Marines. Nobody told us they were leaving. I radioed the other Duster and Quad 50s to stay on 100% alert. It was eerie to look through our Starlight Scope and see no Marines manning their respective positions. Lt. Dan was radioing everyone for assistance and help. *Nobody came or helped.*

July 7: Khe Sanh has become a very lonely place. All of our friends are gone. Lt. Dan and I are on the radio constantly, calling and trying to find out why we have to stay here. I think they thought we left with the other convoys. It's like talking to deaf ears.

July 10: We drove around the base today. We had never been to some of the areas. It was interesting. Nothing was left behind, everything is gone.

July 13: The last few troops from Khe Sanh were loaded on trucks and convoyed back to LZ Stud. Steve Harris and our Lt. Dan took out the first convoy. I was asked to be the rear security on that last small convoy. It was a terrible feeling seeing everyone on that last convoy standing in their vehicles, taking that last look at what was once Khe Sanh. A Marine officer asked if we could drive around the abandoned base looking for stragglers. The Marines, who were short on radios, were afraid that all their men did not get the word to leave. As we drove around the base picking up the stragglers, the NVA artillery gave us their final goodbye artillery barrage. So as not to be caught in the NVA artillery, we loaded the last of the Marines on the last truck in our convoy and instructed them to leave the base and that we would catch up.

I told my men to take a good look and say their personal goodbyes, because we are the last Americans to leave Khe Sanh. We were even nutty enough to stop and take a few pictures and make some personal comments about leaving. Standing on the Duster, we each paid a silent homage to our stay at the famous "Red Clay". The NVA artillery was getting closer and heavier. It was time to catch up to the convoy. I told Earl to put it in high gear; it was time to go home. It was going to be good to get back to Camp Carroll, hot food, showers and seeing our old friends. We have been gone for almost four months.

July 14: I forgot that Steve Harris and I were still on the top of someone's shit list. We only got as far as LZ Stud. I guess we will have to wait a little longer to get our showers and real food. Harris took the north side of the camp, and we had the higher southern slope. We were issued a tent, cots, shovels and picks. An officer I did not know told us to make this our permanent position. The officer ordered us to dig and build a bunker. After we finished, we could get rid of the tent.

July 19:   The ground is so hard that, after five days of digging, we had a hole only about a foot deep and ten feet square. My men, who have already helped fill in by hand an area about a half-mile square at Khe Sanh, refused to dig anymore. Instead, we helped each other make shallow, individual little "graves". We surrounded our graves with sandbags and rocks. During **"INCOMING!,"** we would lay in our graves face up trying to see the enemy shells flying over us, laughing with fear, cursing and yelling "Hit me-Hit me" and praying out loud with Earl. We scrounge each day for building material, so we can build our own above-ground bunker. I don't think we will ever build this bunker and I really don't give a shit.

July 20:   Today I had a visit from two of my hometown friends, John Paulus and Leon Rejman, who were in the Marines. I knew they were at LZ Stud because I would get calls when I was at Khe Sanh that they were looking for me. It was good to talk of home and see old friends, reminiscing of our youth and growing up in good ol' South Plainfield. John and I had played football and hung out together at the Jersey shore. Our minds drifted back to happier times. Hopefully we will spend the next few days together, before we have to say goodbye and get back to the war.

Years later, Leon died from Agent Orange-related cancer. I recently gave his sister, Stella, some old photographs of us from Nam. John owned a few restaurants in New Jersey, fabulous places with great food and service. He has since retired.

July 21:   The Grim Reaper is finally back on "The Road", running daily from LZ Stud to The Rockpile. Ambush Alley is still holding true to its name. The rear deck of our Duster is again stained burnt umber from the wounded and dead. Our hot exhausts smell of burning flesh and blood. We return daily to our shitty little tent, now riddled with shrapnel holes. It is a different existence because we have no consistent means of illuminating the inside of our tent. We have no burning homemade gasoline lights and no electricity. We only have a few candles to see inside the tent, but someone always yells, "Lights out, keep it low, keep it down." Maybe someone cares if we get killed. We surely don't give a rat's ass anymore. Our inner core is drained, and we are running on a reserve of pure hostility and hate.

August 1: I volunteered our Duster to be security for the Marine Medical Unit that visits the Montagnard Village out past the old base called Joliet. It has been months since I have seen these wonderful people. I remembered the last time I was there we ate with the Chief. Sitting around a communal pot in their customary squatted position, we ate some kind of brown soup mixture which I thought was vegetables, chicken, pot belly pig, dog, monkey, lizard and other nameless ingredients. There were very tiny bones in the soup and God only knows what little animals or creatures we ate. Holding various types of bowls to our mouths, we slurped the concoction and nodded with approval. The children thought it was so funny and screamed with joy as I fell over trying to eat and squat at the same time. Not being accustomed to their food, I spent a lot of time on the shitter following our visits.

After all these months, I was surprised the Chief recognized me and greeted me with their traditional bow and a single quick handshake. It was also very noticeable how small the village had become and how few people were left alive. He was amazed and delighted by the NVA skull on my Duster. His smile was a smile of sweet revenge. Climbing on the Duster, he examined it very closely. I wished I could talk to him in his language. We just stood there bowing, nodding, and smiling. The Vietnamese advisor said something to him and he was even happier. Maybe the skull was the revenge he was waiting for. As the Medical Team conducted their examinations, the Chief signaled for me to follow him. At an old kiln that looked like something from the Stone Age, he hand-forged me, from a piece of 55 gallon drum, a beautiful grass knife with a bamboo handle. I looked on in amazement as he made the Vietnamese machete. No one would ever guess it was once a piece of drum. Holding the knife sideways, he bowed and handed me this personal gift. With a slow bow, I accepted this fantastic gift of friendship. Even though we could not communicate, we had a mutual respect and understanding for each other.

His gift is my most treasured possession from the war.

Our Duster guarding the northwest side of Khe Sanh.

Khe Sanh was hit by thousands of enemy artillery shells.

*Daily, the enemy constantly tried to hit our Duster
and bunker with hundreds of artillery shells.*

*Bomb craters from exploded enemy artillery shells
surrounded our bunker.*

Front row: Benny Sitello, Simon Garcia, George Lewis, and
Joe Belardo.Back row: Wally Owens, Earl Holt.
Note how the dirt just clung to us.

A-4 jet that landed at Khe Sanh because of shots in the gas tank.
Notice the fuel leaking onto the runway.

A-4 jet taking off from Khe Sanh.

The burning, crashed helicopter that my crew and I were accused of shooting down.

Private First Class Charles Comanche

Food and supplies being dropped into Khe Sanh by parachute.

NVA artillery shell hitting Khe Sanh.

My new "Grim Reaper" insignia. We called the skull "Ho Chi."

Our Duster getting ready for a new engine.

My crew wanted to get even with me for keeping them at Khe Sanh.

To keep my crew happy, I made them club jackets.
On the back of their flack jackets I drew the new "Grim Reaper":
a skull with 40mm barrels in the eyes and their names along the bottom.

My black eye.

Marine "Ontos"- equipped with six 106 recoilless rifles.

Marine Ontos crew.

Troops waiting to leave Khe Sanh.
Remains of their dead friends are wrapped in the tarps.

Burning cargo plane hit by enemy artillery.

Body recovery.

105mm cannon shooting at the enemy.

The last day of Khe Sanh. My crew made sure the last of the trucks full of Marines left the base. Our Duster rode around the base, making sure they had not forgotten any troops.

The final convoys leaving Khe Sanh.

Duster passing burning Marine Amtrack after ambush on Route 9.

Our new home at LZ Stud.

George Lewis backing up the Grim Reaper into the parapet –
"Her new home."

Hometown friends:
John Paulus, Joe Belardo, Leon Rejman

I said my goodbyes to the wonderful Montagnard
people in the village outside of Joliet.

253

CHAPTER 14: THE SHORT TIMER GOES HOME

August 5: We finally returned to Camp Carroll and have been pre-assigned to the "Water Point" position. We arrived just before lunch and headed directly to the Mess Hall. The last time we had a real hot meal was at Carroll, almost six months ago. Steve Harris and I had our Dusters pull up and park next to the Mess Hall. Charlie Battery guys were assembling, waiting for the doors to open. We were away from base camp for so long that we hardly knew anybody. Most of our friends had already gone home or were dead. All the guys waiting to eat walked over to my Duster and stared at the skull. Wally told them we called the skull "Ho Chi." The men explained that Captain Tedesco always told them crazy war stories of the Grim Reaper crew and their skull. They all thought that he was just trying to get them ready for war and that we were not real. But now, there we were, bigger than life, dirty, smelly, unshaven, with pants full of holes, rolled up above our boots. We must have been some sight. I explained to the guys that we hadn't had a hot meal in months and would appreciate it if we ate first. A few guys got a little mouthy until George pulled out his sword and waved it around. Inside, the cook asked us who we were and did not want to serve us. It was starting to get ugly. Thank God, Tedesco came walking in and explained we were part of Charlie Battery and calmed things down. I spent the first fifteen minutes at the milk machines, drinking a glass of white and then a glass of chocolate and then had several helpings of hot chow. By the time our two crews left the Mess Hall, we had drunk almost all the milk.

It was great seeing Roger Blentlinger again. He welcomed us with a hot shower just for my crew. It was a wonderful feeling having the hot water run over our dirty bodies. I had lost sixty pounds since I left Carroll and needed some better clothes. After our shower, we rode over to the Duster Motor Pool and took fatigues out of the rag barrel. Those were the extra clothes discarded by the men going home and were in a lot better condition than our clothes.

August 8: I am now a short timer and scheduled to leave Charlie Battery, 1st/44th on August 10th. Earl, Wally, and I openly discussed having Earl become the new Squad Leader. George would become the Driver, and they would get a new Gun Bunny. I am becoming very uneasy about leaving. I have trained my men to the best of my ability, but I am not sure if that was good enough. I thought about re-upping. My insides churn with mixed emotions about going home. ***Will they all make it home?*** It isn't the leaving that makes me restless. We have lived and breathed and fought as one team, one unit. I only hope that the "Newbee" replacing me will not let my men down.

August 12: My last day at Camp Carroll was spent in the lookout tower next to the Water Point. I could not help but think of the many battles and all the **"INCOMING!"** and the young men who died in my arms. Before God took them, I learned about their family, friends and pets. I was the last person they would see or talk to. One guy told me he had a pet dog, another, a pet pig, another, a parrot and a cow. They would tell me the strangest things. I just held them tight, gave them morphine and promised I would tell their mothers how brave they were. Nam has been a long year and the view from the high tower sort of puts things in perspective. It is my time to leave the DMZ.

To my surprise, my crew had what looked like a new set of fatigues for me to wear home. George gave me a new razor to shave with, Benny handed me a new bar of soap, and Earl gave me some aftershave and deodorant. After one of Wally's haircuts and another one of Roger's hot showers, I felt like a new person. Before I could leave, my men took turns changing the way I looked, first cleaning off my boots, then blousing my pants, then rolling up my pants, then tilting my boonie hat sideways and finally rolling up the hat edges and sitting it square on my head. They were thrilled with my appearance. There I stood looking like some nerdy geek. Roger boomed in his deep voice "only your mother will love you." They could not stop laughing as they snapped pictures of their prized workmanship.

Captain Tedesco, to my surprise, asked me for my personal night vision Star Light Scope. "Belardo, I don't need to know where you got that scope, and I'm not sure if I really want to know how you got it, but I want it," spoke the Captain. Someone was still squealing on me. "Captain, my boys can't shoot gooks in the dark if you take our scope," I replied. We both smiled and laughed. Tedesco joked, "Joe, all of us can now take turns shooting gooks in the dark. You shot your share. It's time for you to go home." Captain Tedesco was a great officer. He made a difference in our lives, through his true leadership, and was the best Captain that Charlie Battery ever had. I knew he would look after my men. I considered him my friend and knew my men could trust him and his combat judgment. We shook hands and patted each other's backs as we said our farewells. Before I let go of Tedesco's hand, I thanked him and reminded him how my crew would follow him to Hell and fight the Devil for him. I thanked him for not sending me on the Dong Ha Mountain missions. *I always felt that mountain had my name on it.*

I said our traditional "So long, see you later" to all my friends. I was going home. We never said goodbye; goodbye was forever and bad luck. Leaving was an unbearable emotional mental pain. *Part of me has never left my Duster or Route 9.* We would joke and say we knew each other **"When"**. You can add a lot of endings to the word **When**. **When**....nothing you held sacred was sacred anymore. **When**....you thanked God you lived when another died. **When**....you stopped thinking about dying. **When**....you stopped thinking of home. **When**...you............?

In Dong Ha, I was given my unit separation papers and casually handed another Purple Heart with masking tape holding the medal box closed. "We think this is yours, Soldier," the personnel Section Chief said drolly.

Everyone going home from the 1/44th met at China Beach. The officers never knew that we had made arrangements for one of our convoys with about twenty men from Charlie Battery and Headquarters

Battery to meet us at "The Beach." Major parts and supplies had to be picked up at the Da Nang docks. It was an excuse to party for three days. ***China Beach was glad to get rid of us.*** We had taken over the whole place. All of us (Steve Harris, Frank Bardone, Larry Roundtree, John Gunesch, Noble Grinner, Wayne Bailey, Hayden Waite, Paul Raymond and Ray Ellis) were singing, dancing, drinking, eating and acting twenty-four hours a day as if this were our last day on earth. ***It felt great.*** Jim "Doc" Butler was the last to shake my hand. We said our goodbyes because this was a forever farewell. Then we all caught the next plane to Cam Ranh Bay. At the Cam Ranh Bay Departing Center, they gave us a quickie debriefing and shipped us the next day to Fort Lewis, Washington. We left Vietnam singing "Summer Time and the Living is Easy" as Paul Raymond strummed his guitar.

As I flew home in what we called "The Freedom Bird", I could not help but think about my past year: no electricity, limited food (C-Rations), water rationing, hundreds of enemy artillery barrages, occasional bathing, no bathrooms, burning shit, and living with the rats, scorpions and insects. I remembered things crawling on me in our small dark bunker many feet underground, using Agent Orange to defoliate the area around our base positions, friends wounded and dying, taking turns helping at the medical stations and Graves Registration, carrying the wounded, wrapping, tagging and bagging the dead and picking up the pieces, and taking another's life. The small scars on my wrists and on the corner of my right eyebrow would become my daily reminders of extinguishing another human's life. On the plane ride home, I asked the stewardess for a piece of paper and a pen to write my last thoughts of Vietnam.

Dear Diary

My Memories

Zippos, red ants, rubber trees, bamboo, Luckys, Camels, Salems, Pall Malls, Tareytons, Menthols, hedgerow, triple-canopy, re-supply, medic, sulfur, death, mosquitoes, leeches, foxholes, sweating, monsoons, rice paddies, booby traps, elephant grass, trip-wire, fire-support, water buffalos, B-52's, Tet, perimeter watch, Ho's Trail, search and destroy, **"INCOMING"!,** *fire in the hole, dust storms, dust-offs, flares, night vision, infrared, shit burning, outgoing, friendly fire, hot chow, no chow, cold chow, sea-rats, big rats, piss-tubes, chow lines, mail, saddle-up, WIA, MIA, KIA, POW, BNR, corpsman, gunny, mad minutes, spotter round, willy peter, RPGs, AKA's, land mines, toe poppers, punji pits, Montagnards, ARVNS, friendly forces, snipers, sappers, body bags, no bags, green smoke, red smoke, yellow smoke, short rounds, air bursts, diddy bops, real world, my world, short time, long time, no time, make time, medivac, CP, recon, LRRPs, big guns, arc-lights, NVA, Viet Cong, R&R, China Beach, scented letters, mom's cooking, home, live friends, dead friends, no friends, tracers, H&I's, high explosives, full-auto, rapid fire, return fire, single fire, blocking force, L-shaped ambush, malaria pills, Agent Orange, bamboo vipers, cobras, scorpions, spiders, centipedes, rats, Rock Apes, Spider Monkeys, body counts, mass graves, no graves, pieces, 364 days and a wakeup, tracks, trucks, jeeps, Mules, Mighty Mites, wreckers, guard duty, KP, hooch, bunkers, LZ, bros, napalm, 57 recoilless, claymores, choppers, MOS, REMFS, daytime, nighttime, one kill, ten kills, hundred kills, starlight, dig-in, parapets, slit trench, tears, crying, screaming, cheers, joy, laughter, hate, killing, fear, buddies, cold beer, hot beer, no beer, soda, water, hot, dusty, stinky, hot shower, no shower, river bath, helmet shower, no sleep, papa san, mama san, Yards, number one GI, number ten GI, dinky doa, number one boom-boom, Chieu Hoi, ROKs, Aussies, sanctuary, repose, church, prayers, praying, dreams, bugs, darkness, electricity, candles, The Night, C4, lightning, sunsets, mud, red clay, freedom bird, goodbye, later, bouncing betty, .50 cal., bloopers, 175, 155, 105, 106, 40mm, 90mil, 4.2, M60, 81s, M-16, M14, M79, sandbags, ammo boxes, Puff, blood, beetlenut, frag, flak jacket, LAW, flame thrower, rocket launcher, mine sweeps, Dusters, Quads, Searchlights, PRIC-29, PCs, am-tracks, tanks, wire, mine field, nurses, Donut Dollies, round-eyes, generators, lima-lima, SOP, trip flares, convoys, rough riders, make a hole, foul odor, death, lookout tower, we're nothing, they're nothing, ain't nothing, going home,* **NAM.**

As the plane descended toward the runway in Washington, all the men on the plane started screamed with joy. When the wheels touched down, the screams became a roar. One at a time, as we exited the plane, the men dropped to their knees and kissed the ground. It was an emotional experience. Fort Lewis, Washington was nothing special, old barracks with no hot water, traditional military food and everything "hurry up and wait." The military had it down to an assembly-line process. Thirty-six hours later on August 17, 1968, fitted in a custom-tailored dress uniform, complete with new shoes and skivvies, I received my separation papers from the Army. True to the end, my personnel files were all screwed up. I was discharged from the Army with what they call "Temporary Records and a Soldier's Affidavit".

Adding insult to injury, we all missed the last plane out of Seattle and had to sleep overnight in the airport. Several thoughtful men bought us free drinks and food at the airport bar. My family and girlfriend Nancy had no idea that I was back in the States. At first, I thought I would surprise them and just show up on their doorstep, but my friends all agreed that would be too much of a shock and encouraged me to call with my plans. I held my breath waiting for someone to answer my parents' telephone. It was the first time we had spoken in a year. After tears of joy, I told them to meet me at Newark Airport around 5:00 pm the next day. I would be coming in from JFK Airport on a helicopter.

Ironically, I had to take the last step of my journey home in a helicopter from JFK to Newark airport. On August 18, 4:59 PM, I emerged as a civilian, still dressed in military clothes, from the shuttle helicopter at Newark Airport, NJ. As we approached the helipad, I could see familiar faces yelling and waving from the top passenger viewing platform. My family, girlfriend, and a handful of relatives and friends greeted me. I was surprised about how frightened I was about getting off the chopper. I had changed and did not want them to know. It would break their hearts. I never wanted them to know the other Joe Belardo, the Warrior King. After a few restless minutes in the chopper, the pilot told me it was time to go. Like nothing ever happened, I fixed my hat, straightened my tie and put on my sunglasses. This was going to be a mental firefight. Frightened and concerned, I took a deep breath and stepped out of the chopper to meet my family. My father was the first to meet me. We just stared at each other. We both knew the price of war and did not need to speak. He extended his one hand to me and just said, "Well." I removed from my wallet his small red scapula and placed it in his hand and thanked him. "You can have this back when I die," Dad said softly. He hugged me tightly and kissed my cheeks and cried. "Now go say hello to your mother, Brenda, Kenny, Nancy and the rest of the family." I was fortunate, my homecoming was wonderful. I was loved and had forgotten how good it felt.

When we arrived at our house, my father had placed a banner on the front lawn that said **"WELCOME HOME SON"**.

The previous was the last entry in my diary. I was thankful that my tour had ended and that I was welcomed home with the loving open arms of my family and friends.

My mother and father were thrilled when we took down Allen Ginsberg. I came home in time for the South Plainfield Annual Labor Day Parade. The local newspaper asked to do an article about my tour in Nam. The parade was in my name, and I rode with Mayor Gaynor in his Cadillac convertible. It was a great homecoming. The following month my parents had to change their telephone to an unlisted number. The twenty-four hour a day calls never ended. Nameless voices yelling, ***"Baby burner – child killer – rapist – bastard – village burner – war monger,"*** and a hundred other terrible names. My mother cried, and my father questioned my tour. I was never so sad. The war was bad enough. I thought what we read in the papers was journalistic bullshit. I was wrong. My fellow countrymen hurt me more than I can ever express. For years, if I were introduced to someone as a Vietnam vet, the reply would be a single expressive word "Oh". I always wondered what that "Oh" meant. That little word cut me like a knife.

The 1st Battalion 44th Artillery was one of the most highly decorated combat units in Vietnam. It earned the Army Presidential Unit Citation, Army Valorous Unit Award, Army Meritorious Unit Commendation, Navy (Marine) Presidential Unit Citation, Navy (Marine) Meritorious Unit Commendation, The Republic of Vietnam Cross of Gallantry with Palm, The Republic of Vietnam Civil Action Honor Medal and countless Battle Ribbons.

It took years of letter writing before I was reissued my Purple Hearts, Good Conduct Medal, and my other Unit Citations.

Nineteen years would pass before I spoke to an officer from 1st/44th. Out of the blue, I had this overwhelming urge to talk to Captain Easter, Lt. Hardin, and Captain Tedesco. I had left Nam and said my goodbyes to Tedesco, but had never said goodbye or apologized to Easter and Hardin for giving them a lot of trouble. I had to tell them I understood and hoped they would understand. They would know what I meant. I wanted to thank them for getting me home. Maybe without any of us knowing it, they gave us that inner drive to make it home. I know they did what they thought was right and I did what I thought was right. I could not find an address for Easter or Tedesco, but Hardin had signed my New Jersey flag and added his hometown to it. After three calls, I was talking to his mother. I was amazed that she knew who I was. She told me the now Lieutenant Colonel Hardin would love to talk with me. I called the old lieutenant the next day, and we spoke on the phone for almost three hours. Like magic, speaking with Lt. Hardin released my mind and soul from years of Vietnam mental confusion and frustration. It was time for my mind to lock the other Joe Belardo deep in the back of my brain and get on with my life. Talking to the lieutenant was great. I still hope someday to find Captain Easter and tell him I am sorry for giving him so much trouble. He was only doing his best.

He told me he did not know what happened to Easter, but gave me the now Colonel Vincent Tedesco's home telephone number at Fort Bliss, Texas. The good ol' Captain couldn't believe it was me. We spoke for hours. He told me that John Huelsenbeck and Hugh Roberts from the Charlie Battery had started a military club called "Dusters, Quads, and Searchlights".

I went to my first DQS Reunion that year in Indianapolis, Indiana, at Steve Harris' house and was reunited with my "brothers" once again. It had been years since I last seen my friends. I was very nervous and wondered if anyone would remember me. John "Tank" Huelsenbeck was the first Dusterman I would meet from my old unit. Although many years had passed, we did not have to be introduced. It was an amazing "Welcome Home." It was simply "Hi, Tank – Hi, Joey," as we just stood there staring at each other with tears rolling down our cheeks. He turned and introduced me to his wife, Sally, and said, "This is the Joe I've been talking about." Our mental armor fell to the floor unnoticed as we hugged, cried and patted each other backs as Sally wrapped her arms around us, sharing tears with her men finally coming home. The next hugs and tears came from Steve, followed by dozens more as other Dustermen arrived at the reunion. It was as if we had never left Nam.

A few years later, we all gathered at a military reunion at Fort Bliss, hosted by Colonel Tedesco, Colonel House, and Lieutenant Colonel Hardin. The hugs, tears, and stories were the best. The reunion helped us all bury a lot of demons.

In 1989, I started a yearly tradition. Each year on November 10th, we men of the DQS assemble as honorary Marines in front of the Iwo Jima Memorial and participate in the Marine Corps Birthday ceremony. On the 11th we meet at the Vietnam Veterans Memorial ("The Wall") in honor of all our fallen brothers. At the end of the Veterans Day service, we lay wreaths, honoring the men who gave the Supreme Sacrifice serving on Dusters, Quads and Searchlights and as Khe Sanh Veterans. I cannot express the feeling it gives me when we lay a wreath at The Wall. Before the Veterans Day service begins, we leave a small plaque or piece or war memorabilia for our brothers who are inscribed on the wall. Imagine, fifty to one hundred old veterans, standing tall and feeling young, standing in a single line and marching at the half step down the walkway of The Wall. No language is spoken; no calls of cadence are given. The only sounds heard are the footsteps hitting the walkway. The formation stops and in perfect harmony we do a right face, salute and place our right hands on The Wall. A pre-chosen veteran kneels and places a plaque in memory of a fallen Brother. As he stands, all hands come off The Wall and salute as one. The lead person in the line turns and hugs the next veteran in line and says "Welcome Home - pass it down." The Welcome Home is passed down to the very last man. Our Duster Association also has the honor at each anniversary of the Wall to read the names of those who gave the Supreme Sacrifice. I call these two days "The Gathering of Ancient Warriors".

To my surprise and pleasure, several of my personal items left at the Wall are being used in an exhibit of memorabilia which travels throughout the country.

In honor of my journey as a Dusterman, Diane Evans Carlson, President of the Vietnam Women's Memorial in Washington, DC, gave the DQS the privilege of being the Honor Guard at the dedication of their memorial. Five years later, I was one of the guest speakers at their Candlelight Memorial Service. At the Gold Star Mothers' National Convention held in New Jersey, Gold Star Mother President, Judith Young, gave me the privilege of addressing the Mothers in attendance. It was a very humbling and emotional experience.

In 1996, the Air Defense Artillery Magazine did a feature article about the January 24th ambush. Thanks to this article, John "Tank" Huelsenbeck, Earl Holt, Chester Sines, and I were awarded the Bronze Star with "V" for Valor. I had made a promise never to forget Roger Blentlinger, the Marine who risked his life for mine and every other Dusterman and Marine. We refused the medal unless Blentlinger was also awarded the same medal. It was nice that we all finally got some recognition for our service to our country. It was even a better day when I called Roger and told him he was getting an Army Medal. It made a big impression on my family that I was receiving this medal. I was so proud, and it was finally going to give credence to all the Vietnam stories that I had told to my family and friends.

Vietnam would reaffirm my family's teaching that all men are created equal. It is how we treat each other on this glorious planet that separates man from other beasts. **Where** else on earth could men or women bond in an unspoken brotherhood? **Where** else on earth, regardless of race, color or creed could you share a can of food with one spoon for five people? **Where** else on earth could you share the intimacies of families, friends, religion and politics and be willing to die for each other without question? **Where** else on earth could you share your inner most fears, witness men in their glory, and help them through their deepest sorrows? **Where** else on earth are you stripped of everything you consider holy and do things you never thought you were capable of doing? **Where** else on earth do you really hope God will forgive you? **Where** else on earth do they send you home and have you start your life all over like nothing ever happened? These were the best of "Life's Lessons" you could ever learn and they could only be taught on the combat playing field called "War". Yet, for some strange reason, some people never seem to learn from these lessons.

It was a Hell of a Year and it wasn't until recently that I would admit with great sadness, confusion and pride, the mental cost of being a proud Vietnam Veteran. Maybe it was the year, the time, the turmoil, the homecoming, or the separation from the brotherhood that Vietnam produced. Maybe it was the waiting to be recognized for something that had become a bad dream. Despite all this, and for some strange reason, Nam was **"The Best Year of My Life"**.

Life has its ups and downs. Vietnam filled them both. To this day,
I tell everyone that I was **"A DUSTERMAN"**, one of the
"LAST GREAT GUNFIGHTERS" and damn proud of it.

To all of my Brothers in Arms
"Welcome Home"

265

*Charlie Battery at Camp Carroll had built all new hooches
since I had seen it on April 15, 1968.*

*My last view of the DMZ from the lookout tower
next to the Waterpoint position.*

I said my farewell to my Iron Lady – The Grim Reaper.

My last day at Camp J. J. Carroll.
My crew: Earl, Wally, Benny, George, and my Marine friend Roger
Blentlinger, cleaned me up and dressed me like a nerd.
They gave me the look of Innocence, only a Mother would love.

Here I am in the passenger's seat heading to Dong Ha and home.
My crew escorted all the way.

The party at China Beach, Da Nang.

My Duster brothers at Ft. Lewis, Washington.
Left to right: Noble Grinner, John Gunesch, Steve Harris, Frank
Bardone, Wayne Bailey, Haden Waite, and Paul Raymond.

Sergeant Joe Belardo at Fort Lewis, Washington.

"Welcome Home Son"
To my surprise this sign, handmade by my father, greeted me when I arrived home.
I had forgotten how good it felt to be loved.

VOLUME 1 NUMBER 38
THURSDAY, AUGUST 29, 1968
SOUTH PLAINFIELD, NEW JERSEY
TEN CENTS

Second Class Postage Paid
At South Plainfield, N.J.

NEW JERSEY'S
FIRST NEWSPAPER
PRINTED IN COLOR

THE tribune

Former Army Sgt. Joseph Belardo

His Exclusive Photos

Joe Belardo Comes
Home From Vietnam

Two of his South Plainfield
Buddies are still there

Joe Belardo was a boy of 19 when he was inducted into the Army and when he came home from Vietnam the other day he was a man of 21.

Joe Belardo and Mayor Harry Gaynor in the South Plainfield, NJ, Labor Day Parade.

8 ... THE TRIBUNE, August 29, 1968

NEW JERSEY'S FIRST NEWSPAPER PRINTED IN COLOR

Formerly Suburban Review

119 Hamilton Blvd., South Plainfield, New Jersey 07080
Telephone 756-9000

Published weekly on Thursdays

by

FRAVAN ASSOCIATES

President ... Dom Frasca
V-Pres. ... John F. Van Driel   Business Manager ... James O'Doherty

EDITOR ... PATRICIA FRASCA
Art Director ... Diane Greubel Production Manager ... Lillian Smith
Circulation Manager ... Louis J. Calderone
Advertising Manager ... Michael Kavka   Picture Editor ... Hank Baer
Art & Photo Coordinator ... G. R. Persinger

10¢ per copy $4.00 Sub. per year

Thursday, August 29, 1968

EDITORIALS

Joseph Belardo

We had the pleasure the other day of meeting 21-year old Joseph Belardo, a fine young man who made us feel that America is not raising a lost generation after all.

Joe just returned from Vietnam after a tour of duty with the Army. He is the son of Mr. and Mrs. Joseph V. Belardo of 224 Geary Dr. and should be the pride of any family.

If you're as fed up as we are with the hippies and the phony intellects who have been tearing down America at every turn, we suggest you meet this young man and find out about the other side of the coin. It certainly restored our faith.

South Plainfield can be justly proud of Joe Belardo.

EPILOGUE

Veterans Day, November 11, 1997

I was at The Wall in Washington, DC, with Earl Holt, Wally Owens, John Huelsenbeck, Lt. Steve Moore, and a few others from Charlie Battery. As we slowly walked down alongside the Canyon of Heroes, we rubbed our fingers across the names of old friends and told a brief story about each one. Our emotions were full of memories long forgotten, but now rushing to the surface. As we walked, Wally asked if we could stop at Panel 22W. As we stood there, Wally slowly moved his finger to Line 111 and rubbed his finger on the name of Richard Lee Davis. In a soft whisper, he asked if I ever knew what happened to our Duster C131, "The Grim Reaper." Wally explained that on June 22, 1969, the Duster hit a landmine and Richard Lee Davis was killed, with C131 destroyed forever. We all hugged and cried and exchanged over 25 years of stored-up tears. I could not believe the words he was saying, but down deep inside, I knew they were true. The Track from Hell lived up to its reputation.

I could not help but think, June 21st stateside, is June 22nd in Vietnam. As my family and I celebrated my 22nd birthday and the coming of our first child, a fellow Dusterman, halfway around the world was killed on my Duster C131 - "The Track from Hell." Each year since then, as I blowout my birthday cake candles, I think of Richard Lee Davis and say a prayer.

IN MEMORIUM

> **Richard Lee Davis**
>
> **Panel 22W – Line 111**

About the Author

Joseph Michael Belardo was born June 21, 1947, in Plainfield, New Jersey, to Joseph and Mary (DelliPoali) Belardo. Joe has one sister, Brenda (Ribar). He attended the South Plainfield school system and graduated from the North Jersey School of Design Engineering.

Joe's medals include the Bronze Star w/Valor, Purple Hearts, Army Presidential Unit Citation, Army Valorous Unit Award, Army Meritorious Unit Commendation, Navy (Marine) Presidential Unit Citation, Navy (Marine) Meritorious Unit Commendation, Marine Combat Action Ribbon, The Republic of Vietnam Cross of Gallantry with Palm and The Republic of Vietnam Civil Action, Medal.

Joe and his crew of Duster C131 hold the distinct honor of being the last to leave the finally abandoned Khe Sanh Combat Base. Joe was discharged in August 1968 with the rank of Sergeant E5.

Joe married Nancy (Painton) on December 7, 1968. They have three children: Mary, Joe Jr., and Patrick and four grandchildren.

He has been inducted into the Order of the Four Chaplains and his High School Hall of Fame. Joe has received the State of New Jersey's Distinguished Service Medal and the State's Vietnam Service Recognition Medal.

Joe is very active in the Dusters, Quads, and Searchlights Association; Purple Hearts; Vietnam Veterans of America; Veterans of Foreign War; American Legion; and Disabled American Veterans. He is a past trustee of the New Jersey Vietnam Memorial and Education Foundation. Joe was an original member of Victims of Agent Orange, the predecessor of the first Agent Orange Commission.

His hobbies are fishing and bird watching. Joe is the founder of Support Systems, a custom metal fabrication company. He resides in South Plainfield, NJ.

You may contact Joe Belardo about his book at: **Dusterman6768@yahoo.com**

CPSIA information can be obtained at www.ICGtesting.com
Printed in the USA
LVOW02s0132040915

452710LV00026B/419/P

9 780980 224740